ALL ABOUT

BAR·B·Q

KANSAS CITY STYLE

SHIFRA STEIN & RICH DAVIS

Richard Bylund
Xmas '86

Barbacoa Press
Kansas City, Missouri

Printed in the United States of America

First Printing April, 1985
Second Printing July, 1985
Third Printing December, 1985

ISBN 0-933579-00-4

Library of Congress Catalog Card Number 85-070553

SHIFRA STEIN'S DAY TRIPS AMERICA
Books are available for:
KANSAS CITY
ST. LOUIS
MINNEAPOLIS
CINCINNATI
HOUSTON
BALTIMORE

ACKNOWLEDGEMENTS

No venture ever succeeds without the combined efforts of many people. We've been fortunate to find friends and allies whose input strengthened the production of this publication. Our sincere thanks to:

Contributing writers Tom Bodine, Doug Daniel, Robert Eisele and Connie Sokoloff for their help in compiling the restaurant section.

Photographers Bob Barrett and Norman Pederson for the cover photos.

John Rooker for his endurance, wit and expertise.

Copy editor Deborah Bauer for her eagle eyes.

Judy Hutson, owner of A Typesetter, Inc., for typography.

Lindsay Shannon for his encouragement.

Coleen Davis for gathering and sharing materials on barbecue from around the country.

To our numerous family members and friends for their encouragement, constructive criticism, enthusiasm and love.

FOREWORD

A handbook of just about everything you ever wanted or needed to know about barbecuing, especially a la The Heartland, *Barbecue: Kansas City-Style* offers a wealth of recipes and how-tos for making your own irresistable mouth-smearing creations. Ranging far beyond the expected brisket and ribs, the book includes recipes for fajitas, venison, lamb, chicken, trout, shrimp—even a whole pig! With a few toney numbers like smoked duck and turkey thrown in for good measure.

For those of us apartment-dwellers who are personally barbecue-less, Rich Davis and Shifra Stein offer some mighty fine indoor cooking recipes as well—from barbecuing in your very own oven to those oh-so-necessary side dishes such as beans, potato salads, slaws, cornbread and all that good stuff. And if you have any room left, the book tempts with some real down-home desserts like sweet potato and huckleberry pies. (I personally can't wait to try Thunder Thighs Indian Bread Pudding.)

What this book really does is entice one to hop on the next plane to Kansas City for an orgy of barbecue and beer. Who knows? You might even run into Calvin Trillin at Arthur Bryant's.

Sue B. Huffman
Food and Equipment Editor
Ladies' Home Journal

TABLE OF CONTENTS

INTRODUCTION

Take fresh, thin slices of slowly smoked barbecued beef brisket, pile high on a cushion of plain, white bread and slather with thick, brick-red Kansas City barbecue sauce. Top with another slice of bread and hickory-smoked ham, and crown with more spicy sauce, dill pickles and another slice of bread. This, friends, is barbecue: Kansas City-style. At least four inches high, the triple delight is a party for your mouth.

What Carnegie Deli's classic Reuben is to New York, this sandwich is to Kansas City. Several barbecue joints here offer it daily, along with everything from juicy baby-back ribs to hickory-smoked Polish sausage and mutton.

Most barbecue aficionados agree that without black expertise and influence, this unique American cuisine might never have achieved the popularity it now enjoys. In Kansas City, barbecue flourished in the urban ghettos during the '30s. This was a time when blues and jazz were nearly synonymous with the beef and ribs served up in the backrooms of prohibition-created speakeasies. Most barbecue joints were black-owned and operated and many remain so today.

Some of the best barbecue restaurants anywhere on earth can be found in Kansas City in places long abandoned by white urban city dwellers. Slabs of ribs, mutton, sausage and fresh-cut, unpeeled fries cooked in lard are the hallmarks of this culinary art. Every restaurant carries its favorite style of native Kansas City barbecue sauce guaranteed to bring jaded tastebuds back to life.

Before the '50s only a handful of adventurous whites ventured into black neighborhoods where wonderworks of beef and charred ribs were served in restaurants that offered up a warmth and hospitality as vital as the food.

On Vine, Brooklyn and Highland streets, where boarded-up buildings and crumbled concrete now mark the passage of better days, black entrepreneurs such as Henry Perry, George and Ollie Gates, Charlie and Arthur Bryant, Otis Boyd and John Harris took humble food and elevated it to greatness.

The quality has stayed the same over the years and today the food served at their old establishments gives proof that all great things do not necessarily pass away.

It took the advent of civil rights to get white men to bring their wives and children back to the inner city barbecue meccas. And it took suburban longing for native Kansas City barbecue to encourage restaurateurs to move their authentic barbecue from the urban areas to other parts of the city.

The revolutionary use of the charcoal briquet (created by Henry Ford) made outdoor barbecue a national phenomenon. A wide variety of outdoor equipment encouraged everybody to get into the act. Today barbecue has become such a hot item in Kansas City that its popularity has spilled over past the confines of restaurants, into people's homes and outdoor barbecue competitions.

In Kansas City annual contests have brought out the best competitors in both amateur and professional categories to compete in championship cook-offs that are on par with those of Texas, Tennessee, Kentucky, and the Carolinas.

In fact, barbecue contests are becoming one of the more popular participant sports in the country, and Kansas City is moving up fast on the heels of Memphis and Houston as far as competitions are concerned. Newspaper columnist Mike Royko is hosting contests in Chicago, once considered too far north for good barbecue.

Current Kansas City barbecue contests are being promoted annually by the venerable American Royal, the American Cancer Society and the Kansas City Spirit Festival. At the Lenexa, Kansas contest, barbecue battles are held each year for the Kansas State Championship. (Many of the amateur and professional winners of these contests and their recipes are highlighted in this book.)

"Traditionally women don't seem as eager to enter barbecue contests as men. It is basically heavy physical labor and a somewhat dirty sport that requires endurance, carrying around equipment and getting messy. But that shouldn't stop anybody from trying it."

Carolyn Wells
Wicker's Barbecue Products

For us, watching the emergence of this rediscovered American cuisine is a real treat. We are very excited about Kansas City-style barbecue and feel it is unique enough to warrant special attention. There is so much

---

" People have declared Kansas City the barbecue capital of the United States. There may be barbecue that's as good somewhere, but there sure isn't any that's better."

Otis Boyd
Boyd's Barbecue

---

information about the mystique and mastery of this food that we can hardly contain it all within the pages of this book. What we've tried to do is give you a sampling of the many restaurants and recipes the area has to offer, presenting techniques used by local experts to create their prize-winning culinary masterpieces.

Whether you're an experienced barbecuer or don't know a table sauce from a wet marinade, we hope you'll enjoy the useful and interesting recipes included in this book.

With a short supply of in-depth books on the subject, we feel *Barbecue: Kansas City-Style* will help open up a whole new world for people who love good food. And there may come a day when it will be a household necessity to have at least one bottle of red, tangy barbecue sauce "made in Kansas City."

BARBECUE

REDISCOVERING A UNIQUE AMERICAN CUISINE

Kansas City-style barbecue's most distinguishing feature is its variety. Throughout its early history it has drawn upon many types of woods, meats and sauces to become the most eclectic barbecue in the United States.

We agree that some of the best barbecued brisket around comes out of Texas and outstanding barbecued pork can be found in the Carolinas. But Kansas City has both barbecued pork and brisket, as well as chicken and lamb of equal caliber. We know of no other American city that has this variety of barbecue of such superb quality.

Although this book is about Kansas City-style barbecue, we recognize that there are many varieties of this delicious food throughout the country. To help you understand how barbecue developed into a national pastime and passion we invite you to take a very brief look at its history.

BACK TO THE PITS

Some of the earliest archaeological discoveries, dated around 25,000 B.C., produced evidence of primitive humans cooking meat in small pits. Such findings also indicate that the roasting of game, fish, and other edibles over live coals is humanity's oldest cooking method, preceeding the use of such cooking vessels as pots, bake ovens, and skillets. Even in Homer's *Iliad* outdoor roasting and spitting of hogs, sheep and goats is described.

Long before 1492, native American Indians, primarily in the southeastern part of the United States as well as in the Caribbean islands and areas of northern South America and Mexico, had used a wooden frame, upon which they placed fish and game for preservation by smoking.

Early Spanish explorers to the New World called this framework "barbacoa." The Spanish still use the word to mean a framework on which to store or hang items other than food.

Preservation was particularly important to the Caribbean Indians and natives of the southern east coast because the damp, hot climate made the food spoil quickly. So drying and preserving food on the "barbacoa" was more a matter of practicality than of taste.

One of the earliest American-English adaptations of the word barbacoa was "barbacude." This later evolved into several different spellings, including "barbecue."

As cooking developed in the Southern part of the United States, so did barbecue. It finally culminated in today's open pit barbecues of the Carolinas, smokehouses of Virginia, and closed pit barbecues of Texas and Kansas City.

The popularity of barbecue first became evident as large gatherings of people made the preparation of huge amounts of food necessary. Few indoor kitchens could handle the summertime heat, let alone the logistics of cooking for hundreds or thousands of people.

In the South, as elsewhere, outdoor political rallies and speeches produced huge crowds. To keep the masses happy, food and beverages were served. Various documents from the Colonies during the 1700s indicate that barbecues had become great social and political events.

Numerous comments, and some complaints, also indicated that large amounts of alcoholic beverages were consumed at these gatherings. (Sound familiar?)

All this feasting and fun was part of the unusual festivities at an 1850 Kansas outdoor barbecue where hearty residents barbecued and consumed six whole steers, 20 hogs, and more than 50 sheep, pigs and lambs—about four tons of meat!

None of this, however, would have been possible without the flavorful native woods for smoking.

As with any cooking method, easily available ingredients form the basis for a regional style. Wood for smoking is an important influence in the flavor of the meat.

It's not because hickory or oak, pecan or apple are actually the best wood to use. It is merely a practical consideration as to which wood is most accessible. Whichever wood people grow up with and associate with great barbecue is the best to them.

In the Eastern and Southern parts of the country, oak and hickory are the hardwoods of choice. In the Northeastern part of the country, maple trees and corn cobs abound. In the Northwest, it's alder; the Midwest uses hickory and oak indigenous to the area.

The current craze over mesquite wood comes out of Texas and Arizona, where this ugly, brush-like tree has been the bane of ranchers for decades. But mesquite has found a home in the hearts of barbecuers. One of the hardest woods, mesquite gives off an extremely hot fire and lasts a long time. It also produces an excellent form of charcoal which results in a higher temperature than other hardwoods.

"Part of the reason Kansas City is a great barbecue town is the availability of wood in the area. We've got a lot of it. Out West you don't have as many trees to utilize. There would probably be a lot of cities that would barbecue if they had access to wood."

Frank Hipsher
Porky's Pit Barbecue

Fortunately wood now can be transported from one area to another, making it possible for Kansas Citians to barbecue meats with nearly any wood available in the world. One New York firm regularly packages and ships five different kinds of wood chips. The only drawback to importing wood is the current availability and the price.

VARIETIES OF SAUCES

Like wood, the development of different flavored sauces came about partly through cultural traditions and easy availability.

We take our ketchup for granted. But its origins lie in England where it was a non-tomato, vinegar-based sauce flavored with mushrooms or oysters. The early settlers of Carolina and Virginia brought with them a relative of this sauce and used it as a barbecue baste. Recipes for this type of sauce appear in Colonial writings of the 1700s where vinegar with spices gradually replaced the oysters and mushrooms.

To this day some of the finest pork barbecue ever created comes from the Carolinas, where the whole hog is cooked in an open pit over hickory or oak, while the interior is basted with a spiced vinegar sauce devoid of any tomatoes or ketchup.

Tomatoes were thought by the settlers to be poisonous because they were related to the belladona plant. Tomatoes weren't used in cooking until the 19th century, after one adventurous soul ate a tomato publicly to dispell the myth and probably lived to enjoy the flurry of early American recipes for "green tomato pie" that followed.

The earliest recorded recipe found to date using tomatoes in ketchup is found in an 1824 cookbook. Yet tomato ketchup has become immensely popular only in the past half century in this country. While it remains America's favorite condiment, moving up fast behind it are the tomato-based barbecue, Italian and Mexican sauces.

Since tomatoes were more commonly available in the Inland South and in the Midwest, and because of the availability of Caribbean cane sugars and molasses in the Deep South, tomatoes, molasses and mustard gradually started appearing in the preparation of barbecue sauces.

The popular sauces in Alabama, Georgia, and western North and South Carolina today often are mixtures of vinegar and mustard, or ketchup and mustard, and have a deep red or orange hue. Midwestern and Texan barbecue sauces—as well as those found in some parts of the south—are tomato-based and inherently spicy.

MEATS

Whole-hog barbecue is typical of the Carolinas. Just as dark meat and white meat on a chicken differ in texture and taste, so does fresh pork, ham, shoulder and rib barbecue. In whole-hog barbecue there are some of all of the flavors that come from a mixture of tender meat from the pork ribs, chopped up along with the loin as well as the ham and shoulder. The smoke flavor is minimal, because the barbecuing is usually done over an open pit. Whole-hog barbecue is also cooked with the skin intact which holds in the juices.

As one moves farther west, pork becomes less prominent and beef cattle begin to appear across the ranges of Texas and up through the great plains, just as vinegar sauce gives way to tomatoes going westward. As a result, the most popular and frequently barbecued meats in the Midwest are from beef, although pork and chicken are favorites, too.

"To me, Kansas City is the birthplace of real barbecue. This town is known for pit barbecue—brisket and spare ribs—the genuine stuff. When you chop it up, or mince it, you don't know what you're getting."

Papa Lew Lyman
Papa Lew's Barbecue

THE MYSTIQUE

OF KANSAS CITY BARBECUE

What is Kansas City-style barbecue? The answer probably lies somewhere in the roots of inner city barbecue restaurants which became, from the 1920s on, a melting pot of sauces and traditions brought north to this river town from the heart of Texas and the open pit grills of the Deep South. This background is most likely responsible for Kansas City's famous barbecue sauces.

Further combined with the individual barbecuing techniques acquired on midwestern soil, Kansas City-style barbecue has emerged as a unique yet eclectic food. It is not restricted to the whole-hog pork of the Carolinas, the famous barbecued beef brisket of Texas or the barbecued ribs of Memphis. Kansas City has its own favorites, and when it comes to flavor and quality, it can match the best.

GETTING THE WORD OUT

It took a Kansas Citian to tell the world that barbecue was, indeed, alive and well in the heartland.

When reknowned author and columnist Calvin Trillin left his home town for the Big Apple, he left part of his heart behind at Bryant's Barbecue at 18th and Brooklyn. Over the years Trillin has penned books and magazine stories about his one great love. America finally got his message, and Kansas City was thrust into the national limelight as a barbecue mecca—after having existed as one, long before Trillin exposed the secret.

Because of the quality and diversity of its barbecue, Kansas City's reputation as a special barbecue place is starting to make headlines. We think it's about time.

But what most people don't know is that Bryant's is only one of *over* 60 barbecue restaurants in town! In this book you'll discover some of the better ones, although by no means all of them.

Kansas City barbecue has made missionaries out of visitors and fanatics out of residents, some of whom can't go a week without a fix of smoky, tangy ribs. Some of the urban barbecue joints have moved to classier neighborhoods, attracting a new clientele to an old way of cooking.

Black owners here say they have doubled their business by making the move. Add to this the variety of barbecue establishments owned by both blacks and whites, and you have a veritable profusion of suburban Kansas City barbecue. Yet in most cases it is merely the location—not the food—that's changed.

But there are purists who would never go into a barbecue restaurant that reeks with cleanliness. They resent being served by waitresses in coordinated outfits and hate being forced to listen to Muzak with each bite.

The truth is that formica and grease do not necessarily make great barbecue greater. One should be broad-minded when in search of classic culinary genius.

Some good barbecue does exist in new establishments, just as poor barbecue occasionally is served in "hole-in-the-wall" joints. We hope this book will lead you in the right direction when it comes to choosing some of the best of Kansas City barbecue.

"A big juicy Arthur Bryant's sandwich, or a slab of Rosedale ribs sends me into a food frenzy I can't control. After chewing two or three bites, even Linda Evans in a bikini, calling me for a date, would have to wait."

Larry "Fats" Goldberg
Former Kansas Citian, columnist and author of "The Fats Goldberg Take if Off, Keep It Off Diet Program"

THE "FATHER OF KANSAS CITY BARBECUE"

The evolution of Kansas City barbecue didn't really start with Charlie and Arthur Bryant. It began back in the late '20s, with the advent of a long, lean fellow called Henry Perry. At the beginning of the Depression he moved inside a streetcar barn at 19th and Highland and started barbecuing in an outdoor pit, and serving up slabs of barbecue wrapped in newspaper to make ends meet.

Reputed to be "the father of barbecue" in Kansas City, Perry passed on his style and technique, influencing men such as Charlie and Arthur Bryant, George Gates, Otis Boyd, John Harris and Sherman Thompson—each of whom eventually stamped his own brand of barbecue on beef and ribs.

This legacy of Henry Perry has now become a Kansas City tradition that must be experienced to be understood. And it is this style which makes Kansas City barbecue an experience to be savored.

"Perry's barbecue was new to the city. Mostly it was black people that was buying it."

**Sherman Thompson
Sherman's Barbecue**

Henry Perry

THE LEGEND OF "KING" ARTHUR

It was a gastronomic feast. The world's most famous chefs had arrived in New York in March of 1981 to dine on America's best food and wine. Among the glitterati were such reknowned names as Paul Bocuse, Wolfgang Puck and George Dumas, Pierre Franey and Craig Claiborne. At this 30th Congress of the L'Association des Maitres Cuisineurs de France, there was American cuisine to startle the taste buds: gumbo and red snapper bathed in Creole sauce; Tex-Mex salsa; key lime pie; pastrami; and, of course, Kansas City's contribution: ribs from the reknowned Bryant's Barbecue.

The Maitres fell in love instantly with this special Midwestern food. It wasn't an easy task to import Bryant's spareribs to a New York dinner for 500 people. The law prohibits the shipping of hot food by mail and Bryant's ribs just don't taste the same if chilled and reheated.

The problem was solved by sending a troubleshooter to hand-carry the ribs to New York. The ribs were legally stacked in four first-class seats and carted into the elegant dinner four hours later. Including plane fare, this was one of the most expensive meals on the menu.

How Bryant's ribs made it to the forefront of American cuisine is an interesting story. Arthur Bryant was reared on an East Texas farm. The son of poor farmers, he migrated from there to earn a degree in agriculture in a town called Prairie View. He had the promise of a job in Amarillo, but he never made it. In 1931 he stopped in Kansas City to see his brother Charlie who was working at "Old Man Perry's" place on 19th Street. Perry offered Arthur a job and Arthur stayed. That was the beginning.

Charlie Bryant

Arthur often spoke with reverence about Charlie and Henry being the "great ones" in the business, the ones who taught him all he knew. Many will agree that Perry and the Bryant brothers were a triumvirate of the finest barbecue men who ever lived.

When Perry died, Charlie took over the business and when Charlie retired in 1946, Arthur bought the restaurant and made some cosmetic changes, replacing wooden table tops with formica, and adding linoleum floors instead of sawdust. Later he even installed air conditioning. He never placed much emphasis on decor, saying that "you can't get too fancy, or you get away from what the place is all about."

Arthur Bryant

The one major change he made was the sauce. Arthur once said of Perry that—while he taught him the essentials of good barbecue—he was one "mean outfit." Perry, according to Bryant, enjoyed watching customers gasp as they gulped down water after their first taste of his sauce, which supposedly was one of the hottest ever made.

Arthur wanted to make it "a pleasure" for people to savor his sauce. Having once hinted that his sauce contained paprika, cayenne pepper, salt and tomato puree, rather than ketchup, Bryant settled on a moderately spicy recipe that has lasted to this day.

When Charlie died in 1952, Arthur felt that Charlie's leaving the business was responsible for his death. So Arthur stayed on, first operating out of his building at 18th and Euclid, then later at the present location at 18th and Brooklyn, preparing barbecue from early morning to late at night. There were times he wanted to give it up but, like the barbecue itself, the work was addictive.

The only rest he allowed himself was during the month of January when he gave his employees a month's paid vacation and he took a rest. Then it was back to the pits, cooking up at least 2,000 pounds of U.S. Choice briskets a day.

The beer he served became almost as famous as the beef. Frosty glass mugs stowed in a deep freeze enhanced the flavor of the brew. And the famous, unpeeled fries—still cooked today in lard and sizzled in fat at 400 degrees Fahrenheit—required extra juice from Kansas City Power and Light.

Bryant never married. He said there wasn't enough time. He catered to the people, to kings and politicians, and to writers who spread the word.

Reknowned food critic and *New Yorker* magazine writer Calvin Trillin says in his book *American Fried*, that Bryant's is "the single, best restaurant in the world." When *Playboy* asked Trillin to name what he considered America's three best restaurants, he replied: "Arthur Bryant's, Arthur Bryant's, Arthur Bryant's."

Still, sensitive newcomers to the restaurant were shocked by the same grime and grease that Trillin found so endearing. And only on certain occasions were countermen awed enough to use tongs to handle the meat, such as the time back in 1937 when Emperor Haile Selassie of Ethiopia made a

Doretha Bryant

visit. But, as many aficionados claim, the taste of the ribs is partly the counterman's hand, anyway.

Bryant developed what he termed a "bum ticker" in his later years. In 1982, it claimed his life. There was widespread sorrow and sadness at the passage of this legendary Kansas Citian. His niece, Doretha Bryant, who helped him run the business before his death, was left the restaurant in Bryant's will and took over the reins. Like her uncle, she has done things her way. The floors are cleaner now. There's less grime and grease. The fries are crisper. The beef is leaner. A woman's touch perhaps?

But the old formica-topped tables remain along with the same pit that Bryant used. There still are scores of people who wait patiently in the cafeteria line for the food they crave. The sauce remains as always, its secret still guarded by the petite, soft-spoken heiress of the old-time king of Kansas City barbecue.

OLLIE GATES

When you think of Kansas City barbecue you have to include Ollie Gates and his father, George, who was also influenced by Old Man Perry. George Gates made barbecue his life, starting out in 1945 when he began experimenting with different sauces. In 1949 he found the right recipe and it's been the same ever since.

George W. Gates and a partner bought O'Johnny's Ol' Kentucky Bar-B-Q at 19th and Vine in 1946. Gates later bought out his partner and eventually moved to 24th and Brooklyn, doing business as Gates Ole Kentuck Bar-B-Q. His son, Ollie, began working at the restaurant as a teenager. Eventually Gates moved to a new location on 12th and Brooklyn. In 1958 Ollie Gates left his dad's business to start up his own restaurant, Gates & Son.

Since then Gates has expanded his operations to include five restaurants in various locations around the city (see restaurant section). He's gained national recognition, receiving recent media coverage on the *Today* show when Bryant Gumble won some of Gates' ribs from Jane Pauley on a bet.

Ollie Gates stands six feet three and could pass for a football player, but his expertise is in the field of barbecue. According to Gates, all his meats are bought in huge quantities, and are of the finest quality.

Like Hertz and Avis, Gates and Bryant's draw their own devoted admirers who swear that one place is better than the other. The truth, of course, is totally subjective.

OTIS BOYD

Otis Boyd claims to be the only "complete barbecue man still living in Kansas City," having taken his formal training at a chef's school in Chicago in 1939.

"Don't know anybody else cooking barbecue today that can say that," Boyd claims.

How he has remained one of Kansas City's unsung heroes of barbecue is a mystery. But he had fans as far back as the mid '40s, when he opened his home-style restaurant at the historic corner of 12th Street and Vine—the heart of Kansas City jazz history.

His experience shows in the excellent product he turns out from the grease-encrusted aromatic pit which makes up one wall of the kitchen of his present location at 55th and Prospect. The fragrant hickory smoke fills the room when the pit's big steel doors open. That odor has been a part of Boyd's life for nearly 40 years.

An amiable man in his 60s, Boyd is a walking oral barbecue historian who recalls that when he arrived in Kansas City in 1942, barbecue was still largely confined to urban areas with a large black population.

"Sometime after World War II barbecue began to catch on in the suburbs, too," Boyd says, "especially when people started using backyard grills."

Boyd learned to blend spices for his barbecue sauce from "whatever was around the kitchen." In addition, he takes pride in making his own sausage, which many claim is the best in town. (See Otis Boyd's Sausage in the recipe section.)

RICHARD FRANCE

Richard France has been barbecuing for 40 years. Nearly 30 of those were spent working for Arthur Bryant. Born in Louisiana in 1930, he learned to barbecue as a kid, and built his own outdoor pit. When he came to Kansas City, he got a job at Bryant's washing dishes and, after two weeks, Bryant asked France to help him start "cuttin' and cookin'."

When Bryant died in 1982, France left to open Richard's Bar-B-Q, eventually moving to his present location on E. 50 Highway (see restaurant section).

France has developed his own recipe for sauce, a close relative of Bryant's own. France uses a combination of hickory and oak in his closed pit, smoking ribs five to six hours and brisket 14 to 15 hours. He also serves up mutton—a relative rarity that he smokes at least four hours. He puts out a fine smoked pork tenderloin as well as sausage and chicken. His wife, Corene, is in charge of developing recipes for such side dishes as the special barbecued beans.

Now France's sons are helping him in the business—another barbecue dynasty that should carry on in the same fine tradition as all the rest.

SHERMAN THOMPSON

Sherman Thompson was 21 when he arrived in Kansas City from Arkansas. He recalls that, as a kid, he used to watch his relatives slow smoke ribs and beef over a hickory fire. When he came to Kansas City in 1931, he learned even more tricks of the trade from a cousin who was cooking barbecue in the basement of his establishment at 16th and Woodland.

"At that time my cousin was selling his short ends for 15 cents and long ends for a dime," Thompson recalls.

Thompson also remembers meeting Henry Perry, and being impressed with his food.

"He was a tall, lean man," Thompson relates. "I understand he was the first barbecue man, and the first black man, to start the business in this town. His ribs were good and he sold them for 25 cents a slab. But you didn't get no bread with them.

"Perry's barbecue was new to the city and mostly it was black people that was buying it," Thompson says. "I was just a youngster then. I went by and got his ribs, and took them to a friend's house. We'd have a card game and eat one or two slabs, and have a feast."

The idea of starting a barbecue restaurant stayed with Thompson for many years, but it was 1949 before he opened his own place at 1531 Prospect. (See Sherman's Barbecue in the restaurant section).

"I started experimenting with spices, mixing up what I thought would be a good sauce. I got something I was satisfied with, and stayed with it," says Thompson.

According to Thompson, green hickory wood is the best for barbecuing.

"There's just something about it that does the trick," he says.

Thompson used to sell 1,200 to 1,500 pounds of meat on weekends alone, along with special items like lamb shanks and breast.

The popularity of his food was probably due to the fact that Thompson took great care in its preparation.

"The name of the game in barbecue is good meat, slow-cooking, and good wood," Thompson says.

Thompson also feels it's crucial to be able to tell when the meat is finished and knows when it's ready just by prodding it with a fork.

"You got to know when the meat is ready to come off," Thompson explains. "You can't just walk away from it, 'cause you got to watch your fire. You can overcook and you can undercook. Too much fire and the meat will dry out."

"It's a real art. It's not something just anybody can do."

THE MASTERY

OF KANSAS CITY BARBECUE

Nearly every rule about barbecuing springs from ordinary common sense. The supposed secrets and "mystique" about great barbecue make people somewhat fearful of approaching outdoor cooking.

So here's a chance for everyone to get in on the fun. It's not hard at all, just a little messy, perhaps. Basically all you need is patience, common sense and this book to guide you on the path to better barbecue.

GRILLING VERSUS BARBECUING

In Newark, New Jersey, a misguided young man invited dinner guests to a backyard "barbecue," serving them charred steaks cooked over an open flame. When that same man moved to Kansas City, he learned that he'd committed a common error by referring to grilled foods as barbecued.

"I always thought barbecue meant cooking steaks on the grill," he admitted. "When I came to Kansas City, I found out differently."

He wasn't alone in his delusion. There are many who confuse barbecuing and grilling, thinking that quick-cooking hamburgers on a hibachi is barbecuing.

There is a distinct difference between the two. Grilling is done quickly, and meat is seared fast to maximize juice retention. Steaks, chops, hamburgers, fish and marinated chicken work well for this method. The high and direct heat produces fast results, sealing in moisture and cooking the food quickly before it toughens. Grilling is like frying or sauteing, just as barbecue is similar to roasting.

BARBECUING VERSUS SMOKING

The Chinese method of "cold smoking" various meats is excellent, but it isn't barbecuing. Cold smoking is related to the native American Indian way of preserving meats—the same methods used today by the smokehouses of Virginia.

The fire, coals or wood are at a distance from the meats that are hung on open racks, so that the smoke does not cook the meat.

Such meats can be smoked many hours, often hanging for more than a day in the cold smoker. Some old-time methods called for three weeks of smoking. If these meats were used immediately, they would be inadequately cooked and tough. The majority must be baked in the oven or cooked in some additional way, with salt-cured foods soaked in water first.

Barbecued foods, on the other hand, are both smoked and cooked. Adhering to the following principles is important if you want to make the most of your time and money when you prepare genuine Kansas City barbecue.

IN THE BEGINNING

Barbecuing Kansas City-style is like learning how to drive a car. Once you've got the basics, the rest is easy.

To begin with you'll need the right type of equipment and a knowledge of the varieties of grills you can use. By reading the manufacturer's directions, you'll learn how to maneuver the air vents, adjustable grids, fire pans and covers.

To make the job easier, we've included some brief information on grills, accessories and tools.

BARBECUE UNITS

These range from gas grills, hooded braziers and square-covered cookers to water smokers, portable grills and kettle cookers—not to mention the home-made varieties. If you aren't a do-it-yourselfer, you can choose from brands such as Hasty-Bake, Weber, Willingham or other units.

The right unit depends upon your lifestyle and the type of cooking you plan to do.

The Open Brazier

THE OPEN BRAZIER—This is really nothing more than a shallow metal pan with a grid on top. Some braziers have half-hoods, covers or battery-operated rotisseries. Tabletop hibachis are also considered open braziers. These are perfect for grilling hamburgers, steaks, poultry and fish but are not suited for serious slow smoking.

Covered Cooker

Japanese Kamado

COVERED COOKERS—These come in all shapes and are quite versatile. When you take the cover off, the smoker acts as a grill. These types of cookers come with adjustable firepans or grids, and vented covers for controlling heat. With dampers to control fire temperature, you can cook larger pieces of meat. When the cookers are covered they can be used to barbecue.

While covered cookers usually come with a thermometer in the lid, they aren't always dependable. It's better to have a regular meat thermometer to avoid mistakes. You can also adjust the distance between the food and coals by raising or lowering the fire grate. Some models also have a fire door that allows you to add more fuel without opening the top.

Expensive wagon models are usually made of heavy metal with a heat-resistant finish. You can buy accessories for these, including rotisseries, extra grills and smoking equipment.

THE KAMADO—This type of oven is becoming quite popular. It is ceramic and looks like a big egg, with the small end flattened to make it stand upright. It boasts a controllable smoke vent and draft door. The top third acts as a lid. When the lid is open, you can grill. Closed, the smoker becomes an excellent oven.

A firebox at the bottom has an iron grate to contain the charcoal. You can barbecue with charcoal alone or use hardwood chips in addition. There is a Chinese oven similar to the Kamado, but barrel-shaped rather than looking like an egg. Both have inspired people who want to make their own ovens, using the pull-out firebox technique which makes it easy to add charcoal in small amounts throughout the cooking process.

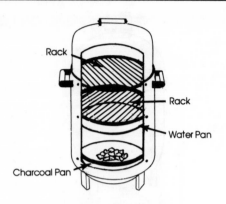

Rack

Rack

Water Pan

Charcoal Pan

Charcoal/Water Smoker

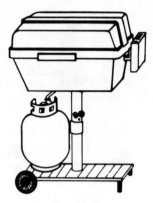

Gas Grill

WATER SMOKERS—These have heavy dome-shaped tops and a built-in water pan. Many outdoor enthusiasts use these ovens for cooking game and fish.

You can slow-cook your food in these ovens, flavoring them with your favorite woods and letting the meat automatically baste and bathe in the moisture. But some serious barbecuers don't like this method because the meat is permeated by the water and doesn't get the hard, crusty finish it does with dry smoking.

"If you use a water smoker, only put water in your pan. Anything else adds flavor to the meat, and you don't want a brisket to taste like hot beer."
John Schlosser
Head Chef, Cowtown Cookers

GAS GRILLS—The idea of gas grills might insult traditionalists who rail at the idea of smoking without charcoal, but these ovens are quite popular and more economical to operate than charcoal barbecues. They also are ready to use in a short time and cleaning is a breeze. However be sure your unit is capable of producing the low temperature settings necessary for slow cooking.

There are adjustable gas grills where you can shut off the heat to one side to allow for a cooler area to cook the food. However, the fire source and the grill are usually at a fixed distance from each other.

The actual taste you get from cooking with gas comes from the flavor of the smoke produced by the fat dripping onto the volcanic lava rock. You can also sprinkle water-soaked hickory chips on the rocks to enhance the flavor if the manufacturer's directions permit. Whether or not this is barbecue depends on your definition of the subject.

HOME-MADE SMOKERS—There are those inventive and intrepid enthusiasts who much prefer to make their own smoke ovens. In Kansas City everything from refrigerators and barrels to electric cookstoves and cement blocks are in constant use in people's backyards and at barbecue contests. If you are serious about the subject, you might want to investigate making your own. While we can't give you all the instructions in the limited space of this book, we can recommend you attend some national or regional barbecue contests where these types of smokers are in use. Some contestants offer their homemade devices for sale. Others sell instruction kits.

There are several requirements to building an efficient smoke oven: a fire pan to create heat and smoke; an area to confine the smoke; racks or hooks to hold the meat; an adequate draft and controllable air inlet near the source of the smoke; and air outlets at the top of the smoker, if possible.

Here are a few of the people in Kansas City who've come up with their version of the perfect smoker.

PAUL KIRK'S "THE PIG" (THE 55-GALLON DRUM)

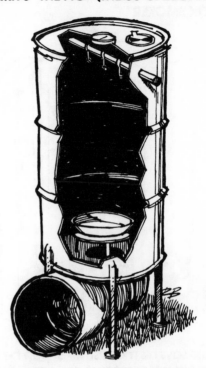

This variation on a chemical-free 55-gallon drum can smoke 22 slabs of pork ribs or 90 pounds of brisket at one time. The pig smoker may be purchased fully assembled with instructions and recipes. You can also get easy-to-follow plans to build it yourself. For information write The Recipe Exchange, 3625 W. 50th Terr., Shawnee Mission, Ks. 66205.

JOHN "BUFFALO" GATTENBY'S "ICE BOX SMOKER"

Buffalo says his meat smoker can be built from an old refrigerator of any size. Refrigerators are well insulated and hold heat, save fuel, and offer a full-length door that's convenient for loading and unloading. To convert a refrigerator into an oven takes some work and we definitely don't advise building one yourself, unless you've talked with experts. You can find them at barbecue contests and cook-offs around Missouri. (WARNING: Old refrigerators can be a hazard for small children and may contain residues of freon gas).

AL BOHNERT'S PIG PIT

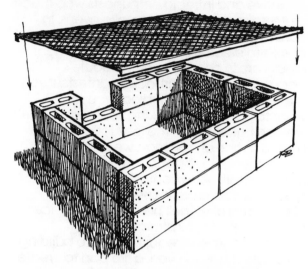

A smoker oven can easily be made of standard cement blocks using a level, firm foundation. No mortar is necessary since the pit is designed to be semi-permanent. Above is Bohnert's design for a grand pit designed to feed people who tend to make hogs of themselves. It's the one he uses when he competes at barbecue contests.

BRUCE "DOC" DANIEL'S "SMOKER DELUXE"

Doc Daniel's smoker is a stripped upright freezer which he claims puts out some of the best barbecue in Kansas City. It's got removable racks, and a steel firebox to boot. The same precautions apply here as when converting old refrigerators.

LINDSAY SHANNON'S SUPER SMOKER

Barbecue enthusiast Lindsay Shannon built his smoker from a 55-gallon drum and turned it horizontally, using bicycle handle bars to maneuver it.

OTHER FORMS OF HOME-MADE OVENS include old electric cookstoves, chemical-free barrels and outdoor smokers built of bricks and mortar.

ACCESSORIES

To produce good barbecue, you'll need the right accessories. It's essential that you have tools that are easy to clean and handle. A utensil rack on the grill keeps them nearby.

Meat Thermometers—these come in handy for large cuts of meat that may not get done on the inside without some sort of meat probe.

Tongs—you'll need two sets: one for coals, the other for food.

Long-handled metal spatula, fork and basting brush—the spatula turns the food, the fork spears the veggies and the basting brush brushes the sauce on the meat during the last hours of cooking time.

Gloves, mitts or hot pads—these should be heavy duty and able to withstand high temperatures. It's preferable to use extra long mitts for handling hot grills and avoiding splatters.

Spray bottle for water and baking soda—to extinguish flare-ups.

Charcoal starters—these can be the electric, liquid or chimney type.

Hinged grill baskets—ideal for turning foods such as fish, hamburgers, or pork chops.

Long handled skewers—perfect for kabobs.

STARTING A PROPER FIRE

Knowing the number of ways and products available to start an outdoor fire for barbecuing goes along with learning the principles of good barbecue. Here are several methods:

1. NEWSPAPERS AND KINDLING. One of the most common and simplest ways to start your barbecue is the way people have started fires in their fireplaces for generations.

Twist some newspapers into long log-like links. Make two crossed layers of wadded-up newspapers. On top of them, place small pieces of twigs for dry kindling. For hardwood-cooking fires in big pits use small logs, or add charcoal briquets on top of the kindling in order to ignite the charcoal.

Light the edges of the newspapers on all sides. If the fire has been built properly, before long the charcoal will begin to get white.

One disadvantage of this type of fire is that unless it is built with a slight indentation in the middle of the newspaper-kindling area, the charcoal will scatter about the cooking unit as the paper and twigs eventually burn away. This is why this method is a less effective way to start your fire than some of the others described.

2. ELECTRIC FIRE-STARTERS. A simple way to start a fire is by using an electric fire-starter. Place it in the center of your cooker, and pile the briquets on top according to the manufacturer's directions. When the briquets begin to turn red (around 10 or 20 minutes, depending upon the unit and the outdoor temperature) you can turn off the electrical apparatus and remove it when cool.

The major hazard here is forgetting about the unit and having it get too hot, thereby damaging it, or the oven. Inserting a timer between the electrical outlet and the plug for the starter probably is a good idea. Set the timer according to the instructions on the electrical starter.

Each electrical fire starter should have its own instructions you should carefully follow.

3. LIQUID FIRE-STARTERS. Never use kerosene, gasoline, or quick-igniting fuels when starting a barbecue fire. Instead, start your fire by stacking 12 to 20 briquets in a pyramid in the center of the cooker, then spray on a liquid fire-starter specifically designed for barbecuing. These commercial preparations have a much lower flashpoint and are much safer.

However, the disadvantage of this method is the lingering odor that can attach itself to the food. If the food is put on before the charcoal ashes down, chemical fumes can ruin the flavor of the meat. The fire also can go out if you use too small an amount of starter fuel.

Never try to restart a fire that already has been lit by trying to douse the coals with more fuel. This is dangerous since there still may be live coals that can flare up and burn you. Liquid fire-starters are meant to be used on charcoal *before* it is ignited.

If proper precautions are taken, this is a safe means of starting your fire.

4. FUEL-COATED SUBSTANCES. These range from fuel-soaked barbecue briquets to wood products or sawdust compressed into sticks that include an igniter fluid. These fire-starters can be inserted in the middle of the cooker and the briquets piled on top. You light a match to these and with adequate ventilation they catch fire and burn long enough to ignite the charcoal before burning themselves out. Again, fumes and odors can result from this method, unless the chemicals burn down completely before food is placed on the grill. Sometimes coated products don't catch on fire as easily as liquid fire-starters, particularly if they are old or have been left uncovered for a while.

5. THICK, JELLY FIRE-STARTERS. These are considered safer than liquid fire starters, although they have never been quite as popular for some reason. Simply spread over the charcoal and light.

6. METAL "CHIMNEY" FIRE-STARTERS. This is probably the best, safest and cheapest method of all. The "chimney" is simply a round piece of metal about six to 12 inches in diameter and eight to 15 inches high, much like a large tin can with both its bottom and top removed. A chimney fire-starter has the advantage of never having a chemical odor or taste to impart to the food. There is also no cost of fuel source, other than charcoal.

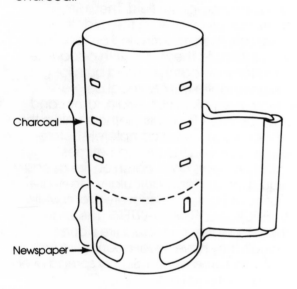

Chimney Fire-Starter

There is a lattice-like insert toward the bottom of this unit that holds charcoal in the upper portion. Below this, you insert crinkled newspaper which serves as the fire source. Punctured holes around the bottom allow ventilation as the newspaper burns and ignites the charcoal above. Once the coals are reddish in color, they can be dumped out into the barbecue unit.

Make sure your unit has enough space to enable you to utilize the chimney effectively. One disadvantage here is that there is usually a handle on this device for charcoal removal. The handle can be quite hot so be sure you get one that's insulated, or wear gloves.

7. BUTANE, NATURAL GAS AND ELECTRIC OUTDOOR GRILLS. These cookers can be lit automatically or with a match and the heat source made instantly available. The advantages are obvious. There are those who prefer these types of grills simply because little clean-up is necessary and no chemical starters are needed.

However, these grills lack the natural flavorings that come from hardwood charcoal and soaked chips. Some manufacturers say that you can add soaked chips to their units to help the taste. Be sure to check first, since ashes can plug up the tiny gas vents.

But true barbecue pros shun such artificial devices. There are heated arguments among the professional restaurant barbecuers as to whether it is genuine barbecue if one uses gas to ignite the fire of hickory or oak logs.

8. SAFE STARTS. In general, starting a barbecue fire, with a source of heat intense enough to ignite the charcoal briquets, is a simple procedure. Follow the instructions carefully for each method previously discussed and you'll be able to start a fire safely.

Ordinary precautions about where the fire is built, how far away it is from the house, and whether or not there are small children or pets nearby are certainly necessary considerations when barbecuing outdoors.

It also makes sense to avoid firing up the grill near valuable shrubbery or underneath a low-limbed tree. Just look around you and be sure you've done everything necessary to ensure your barbecue turns out to be fun and enjoyable. Exercise good old common sense, and you should have no problems at all.

9. JUST IN CASE. If you have a flare-up don't panic. This usually indicates your fire is too hot for closed-pit barbecuing. It could also mean that the meat is directly over the briquets and dripping fat into the fire. Be sure to have a ready means of dousing the flames fast without reducing the heat. A plastic plant sprayer works well in emergencies. Be careful to spray the water on gently so it won't shower the meat with ashes.

As pointed out earlier in the book, there are many varieties of woods used for grilling and smoking meats. Since we are talking primarily about barbecuing and not grilling, we'll discuss woods commonly used in Kansas City-style barbecue. But first it's important to know what different sizes of woods can do.

CHIPS, CHUNKS, AND SAWDUST. There is a distinct difference in the utilization of wood products for barbecuing. Hickory and other woods in the form of sawdust or small chips burn fast when placed on the grill. So it's important to soak them in water at least 30 minutes before using. This cut of hardwood provides immediate results, imparting a light, smokey flavor that enhances a quickly-seared steak or other food that doesn't need cooking for a long period of time. These fine particles of wood then are used for grilling, not true barbecuing.

In barbecuing, when you need smoke produced over several hours, you'll want larger chunks or even small pieces of wood logs that have been soaked in water for several hours. Many barbecuers advise letting the largest chunks soak at least 24 hours, so choose your size depending on purpose, just as you need to select varieties of woods for their particular flavors.

HICKORY. Hickory is probably one of the most popular woods in the United States for barbecuing. It's available in diverse sections of the country and is also an excellent hardwood that burns slower than the softer woods to produce an excellent smoke flavor. However, too heavy a hickory smoke over a long period tends to turn foods bitter. This is also true of mesquite or other woods.

Hickory wood is fine for smoking meat from turkeys to brisket, pork and goat. If you're lucky enough to live in an area where hickory is a native wood, you can even build your fire using small hickory logs. Just make sure your cooker can be closed down enough so that you're mostly heat smoking, rather than cooking with live fire.

Live fire hickory, of course, is excellent for grilling any kind of meat that needs to be seared and cooked quickly.

"The name of the game in barbecue is good meat, slow cooking and good wood."

Sherman Thompson
Sherman's Barbecue

MESQUITE. This wood has been around forever in the Southwest and recently has increased in popularity. One of the hardest woods known, it produces a distinct, smoky flavor.

Mesquite charcoal produces the high temperatures necessary for searing meats and sealing the juices inside and thus is better for grilling than barbecuing.

The flavor of mesquite, like hickory, can become bitter if you smoke it over the fire for too long. However, barbecued brisket has been cooked as long as 20 hours using mesquite, with delicious results. It all depends on the control used to vary the amount of smoke and temperature, as well as the preparation of the foods to be smoked.

The cooking temperature for mesquite is often as high as 900 to 1,000 degrees F. or higher. The mesquite charcoal is rather smoky and has a habit of popping little fine sprays of red sparks as it continues to heat. If you're using mesquite for the first time, don't worry. This isn't a sign of an inferior product— just a sign of good mesquite charcoal.

Among the first to use mesquite to sear fish and other foods were Jonathan Waxman, who left Santa Monica to open Jams restaurant in Manhattan; Wolfgang Puck, chef-owner of Spago and other restaurants in Southern California; and Alice Waters, chef-owner of Chez Panisse in Berkely, California. Since then many restaurants have installed mesquite grills to produce this unique flavor.

FRUIT WOODS. Most of the common fruit woods are considered excellent for barbecuing. The most popular and easily available are apple, peach and pear. Lately grape vines and clippings have also been used. Cherry has a good flavor when mixed with other woods, although it's generally less available than most. If you're lucky enough to have a contact at a local fruit orchard, you might ask if, after the trees are pruned, you could keep the clippings, which are excellent sources of smoke.

Smaller clippings can be tossed on the grill when cooking hamburgers or steaks. Soak the larger chunks in water and use them in straight barbecuing.

MAPLE AND CORNCOBS. This combination is commonly used in the Northeastern part of the United States, where there is easy access to both. The excellent flavor they produce has been imparted to some of the famous hams and Canadian bacon that come out of Vermont.

ALDERWOOD. This is a superior wood for smoking. It is used in the Northwest and is not readily available in the Kansas City area.

SASSAFRAS AND SASSAFRAS ROOT. The good news is that this is probably the best flavoring wood to use for smoking. The bad news is that it's hard to obtain. In addition, certain chemicals contained in sassafras tea are considered health hazards, although no specific studies we know of have been done on the smoking of foods with sassafras wood or root.

Over the years, one Southern Missouri family-owned smokehouse has produced fine prize-winning bacons and hams smoked with this exotic root. Plenty of folks have consumed these meats without any apparent health problems. But without conclusive evidence either way, it's difficult to assess the safety of this wood for barbecuing. The flavor, however, is sensational.

PECAN. Pecan seems to be the principle wood from the nut-bearing trees that has gained popularity. It's hard to find, and only certain parts of the South seem to have pecan trees in abundance. Pecan, along with the other woods mentioned, are current favorites of Kansas City barbecuers. Pecan smoked foods have a particular delicate flavor. In addition pecan doesn't seem to produce the sooty residues that other woods woods do.

CHARCOAL— THAT OLD BLACK MAGIC

Perhaps as early as 300,000 B.C. somebody discovered that charred wood burned better than uncharred wood and prehistoric man may have looked for ways to make more of it. Eventually someone covered fire with earth to prevent complete combustion and lo, the art of making charcoal was born. Today, however, the majority of those who do outdoor cooking far prefer the use of charcoal briquets to the lump charcoal used by our prehistoric ancestors.

Yet briquets were rarely used before World War II except for commercial uses. It took Henry Ford to turn the charcoal briquet into a household necessity.

In the early '20s, Ford couldn't buy wood alcohol, except at very high prices. The Ford plant badly needed alcohol to use in the manufacturing of automobiles, so Ford brought in a chemist who proceeded to come up with a grand idea for wood distillation.

A modern plant was set up and 80,000 acres of woodland purchased for the venture. The Ford Chemical Plant was equipped with everything to chip, char and dry wood. Soon alcohol by the carloads was being generated from wood distillation. There was, unfortunately, the troublesome by-product of charcoal to deal with. Henry came up with yet another idea: why not make one uniform product of charcoal and sell it all over the country?

Automatic briquetting machinery was installed and the new Ford Charcoal Briquets soon were coming off the presses every day. Among the first to realize the potential and long-burning qualities were foundries, then hotels and restaurants who realized that briquets were an excellent medium for broiling.

Today the availability of charcoal briquets has made outdoor cooking a national pastime. As consumers have discovered, the quality of charcoal briquets can vary greatly.

Most briquets are a blend of hardwood charcoal with anthracite or sawdust, a lighting ingredient, and starch binders. The greater the percentage of hardwood charcoal, the better the charcoal briquet.

According to John Uhlmann, whose Kansas City-based company manufactures Patio Chef Charcoal Briquets, there are several things to consider when purchasing briquets.

 "The charcoal needs to light in a reasonable period of time and should be 80 percent ashed over and ready to cook in at least 30 minutes," says Uhlmann. "It should also reach a minimum of 425 degrees within 30 minutes and be at 350 degrees or hotter for at least one hour."

Uhlmann points out that the flavor you taste is actually caused by the wood charcoal in the briquets. These volatiles or flavor agents are in the wood itself which is what is captured as the wood is converted into charcoal.

"It is important to remember to let the coals get at least 80 percent ashed over to avoid the taste of lighter fuel," Uhlmann says. "Too often people start cooking before the coal is properly ashed. The charcoal must be hot enough, or you can get the chemical taste of the fluid in the meat."

MISSOURI HARDWOOD IMPORTANT TO KANSAS CITY'S BARBECUE SUCCESS

Missouri is the nation's largest producer of hardwood charcoal and charcoal briquets. Indeed, the availability of Ozark hardwood—hickory wood in particular—is an important ingredient in Kansas City's barbecue success. But it takes more than charcoal briquets to produce a hickory smoked flavor. There are many barbecuers who put hickory chunks over hickory-based charcoal to get a stronger flavor. The same holds true for mesquite charcoal and chunks. However, it is easier to control the temperature of charcoal, than wood.

Whether or not you use charcoal or gas to cook, bear in mind that almost every barbecue contest winner prefers to cook with charcoal and considers this form of fuel the "black magic" needed for cooking barbecue at its best.

"People use too much charcoal when they barbecue. Use small amounts at a time and continually refuel."
Dick Mais
Barbecue contest winner

LIQUID SMOKES, DRY RUBS, WET MARINADES AND SAUCES

LIQUID SMOKE

There are many varieties of liquid smoke, including hickory and mesquite-flavored products. While not particularly loved by the serious barbecuer, nevertheless they come in handy when you can't cook outdoors.

Made by burning the wood itself the liquid smoke is processed and filtered through water and harmful ingredients extracted from it. Approved by the FDA, liquid smoke works well for barbecued beans, indoor ribs and brisket, but it can't substitute for a table sauce, and it shouldn't be used "raw" since it has a bitter taste.

Liquid smoke can be combined with water, in a ratio of two parts water to one part liquid smoke, and the meat marinated in this solution for 30 to 60 minutes. Remove and cook the food in the usual manner. You'll notice that there is a reasonable facsimile of smoke flavor, although it really doesn't come close to an honest-to-goodness hunk of outdoor barbecued beef.

Note: To marinate meat in a liquid solution, always use non-corrosive glass, stainless steel, ceramic or plastic containers, including heavy-duty, sealable plastic bags. Never use aluminum or other metals. Place in refrigerator and turn occasionally.

DRY RUBS (also called dry marinades)

Marinate means to soak in a liquid that is often vinegar- or wine-based and enhanced with spices. This way you can both tenderize and improve the flavor of the food. Although "dry marinade" is rather a contradiction in terms, it still is used frequently to describe a mixture of barbecue spices that are rubbed on meats before cooking.

Dry rubs are also excellent for indoor barbecuing. Some of them also include powdered smoke, making it possible to get outdoor wood flavor, a passable imitation of the real thing.

There are some people who use dry rubs on everything. You can make your own concoction, but it takes some practice. (Also see wet and dry marinades in the recipe section.)

Three basic ingredients often used for dry rubs include salt, paprika and brown sugar, followed by varying amounts of chili powder, garlic powder, pepper and other spices such as cayenne pepper (if you can stand the heat.)

Other ingredients such as cumin or powdered mustard add to the list of endless possibilities.

However, barbecue contest winner Dick Mais cautions against the use of salt.

"I never, ever use it on red meat," he says emphatically. "It's a natural toughener and will dry the meat out if you plan to cook it slowly." (There are barbecuers who would argue with Mais, many of whom use a mixture of salt and sugar to win barbecue competitions.)

On the other hand, Mais is a big fan of such spices as sage and sweet basil. He adventurously adds sage to the marinade when he cooks beef to give it a "wonderful, exciting flavor." He also insists that sweet basil, brushed on after applying a dry rub, will enhance the taste of lamb considerably.

It all boils down to the method of cooking. If you cook at a higher heat, over a long period of time, then a great deal of fluid can be extracted from any food. Slow cooking at a low temperature forces less juice out of the meat that is sealed with an external dry rub.

The searing process, itself, tends to seal any food that is cooked fast on a grill, such as steaks or hamburgers, preventing fluid loss.

An example of this is the famous "blackened red fish" recipe created by chef Paul Prudhomme of New Orleans. Imitated now in many parts of the country, the dish is prepared by applying spices and seasonings to the fish, which is then grilled in butter at an extremely hot temperature, on a metal grill, such as an iron skillet. The fish is seared to a blackened state on the outside, yet remains moist and tender inside.

Often cooks will utilize a thin layer of prepared mustard before applying a dry marinade. The mustard contains vinegar, which is a natural tenderizer. A mustard that is both hot and sweet works well with a rub that includes brown sugar and paprika. The dry marinade may contain garlic which further seasons the meat.

Dick Mais slathers on mustard for his pork loins before barbecuing (see his "Honey-Smoked Pork Loins" in the recipe section.) He adds his own brand of dry rub and turns on the low heat to break up the brown sugar. When halfway through the cooking process, he bastes the meat with a mixture of honey and spices. Mais says the honey "crystallizes in the pores of the meat and locks in the juices."

While there are some chefs who swear by the paprika/brown sugar and spices combination, there are those who cook ribs, chicken and pork using only pepper or nothing at all. They insist the taste comes from the ultimate control of the temperature and smoking process.

WET MARINADES

According to Webster's Dictionary, one definition of barbecue is to "cook in a highly seasoned vinegar sauce."

Not that everyone would agree. Many purists would never barbecue with mixtures of beer or soy sauce, nor do they use stovetop blends of butter and wine. These mixtures aren't like the blends of peppers and spices used for barbecuing. And, while oriental-inspired sauces may produce an excellent taste, just don't confuse them with traditional American barbecue.

Many people don't realize there is a definite difference between dry and wet marinades and red tomato-based table sauces. It's like comparing apples and applesauce. Each is wonderful in its own way but distinctly different.

In states where barbecue is a way of life, dry marinades and table sauces often complement each other.

Traditionally wet marinades are vinegar-based, spicey mixtures that tenderize the meat and cook through it, instead of burning onto it. Many people baste the meat the last 30 minutes with a red sauce to give it a crusty glaze. The red sauce is usually offered at the table. (It should be noted that, in some circles, putting a red sauce on a hickory-smoked marinated chicken may be viewed akin to putting mayonnaise on Peking Duck.)

Wet marinades are occasionally used in such states as the Carolinas, Arkansas, Tennessee, Mississippi, and Kentucky, and in other areas of the south.

Many people make their own wet marinades using a blend of oil, vinegar and spices. Some add vinegar to packets of dry marinades and others simply buy it ready-made.

The beauty of wet marinade is that it can make tougher cuts of meat, such as flank and round steak, and brisket taste like a rich man's bounty. It also works well for pork, chicken, and fish, wild game and beef tenderloin. The secret is to marinate the meat well, *before* putting it on the grill, then baste it throughout the cooking time.

Our experience has shown that any of the liquid or dry marinades that include tenderizers such as papaya tend to make the meat mushy if it's left in the marinade too long. If the meat is taken out too quickly, the marinade won't have an opportunity to permeate it. Therefore we don't recommend these types of marinades for barbecuing.

SOME TIPS ON COOK
WITH WET MARINA

1. BRISKET—marinate overnight, then cook on a slow grill (225 degrees) and baste every 30 minutes with wet marinade until done (around eight hours).

2. PORK RIBS—marinate at least two hours and baste frequently (every 30 minutes) on a low fire (220-225 degrees) for around three hours.

3. CHICKEN—marinate two hours, then cook on medium fire (250-300 degrees), dipping the pieces in the marinade every time you turn them, until done.

4. LAMB—marinate the meat for two hours. You can use the leg, chops or shank. Baste every 30 minutes at 200-225 degrees until done, then finish off with a final squeezing of fresh orange juice.

5. SEAFOOD and FISH—shrimp and trout can be cooked over a low fire and basted every five minutes with the wet marinade until done (around 15 minutes for trout; five minutes for unfrozen shrimp.)

BARBECUE SAUCES (RED TABLE SAUCES)

The quality and style of Kansas City's spicy barbecue sauces are virtually unlimited. A sampling of sauces available in supermarkets and restaurants around the city reads like a local and national who's who of the barbecue business. There are probably more varieties of barbecue sauce available in Kansas City than any other city in the United States. One local supermarket carries over 60 varieties and sizes of barbecue sauces.

Add to this the local barbecue restaurants that sell their sauce on-site, and you've got a virtual Valhalla for lovers of the stuff.

Very few places in the Midwest use the pure eastern Carolinas-style sauce, consisting primarily of peppers in a bottle with pure vinegar, although some of these are available locally.

The majority of successful red sauces are usually variations on the theme of tomato base (in the form of ketchup or tomato puree), chili powder, sweeteners such as brown sugar or molasses, hot spices and the occasional use of liquid smoke.

In the recipe section of this book you'll find outstanding prize-winning recipes for barbecue sauces, as well as dry rubs and wet marinades. But if you'd rather buy ready-made sauce, you're definitely in the right place if you live in Kansas City.

Sauces here provide unparalleled esoterica. Devotees know that they could eat barbecue for a month, and never run out of possibilities.

To show you what we mean, we've included descriptions of some of the better-known sauces available at establishments mentioned in the restaurant section of this book and elsewhere in the text. These are simply our impressions of the flavor, since the actual ingredients are usually kept secret. Some of the sauces are available at the establishments included in our restaurant section. Others through stores, supermarkets and a few by mail order (see Ordering By Mail at the back of this book).

KEY:
Available at restaurant (R)
Available at some stores and supermarkets (s)
Available at most stores and supermarkets (S)
Available by mail order (M)
Available nationally (N)

BOBBY BELL'S: Nicely balanced with herbs and mild spices in a tomato base, with a touch of honey to bring out the flavor(R,s)

BOYD'S: Tart with anise, chili powder and a hint of cinnamon. (R)

ARTHUR BRYANT'S: Grainy with paprika and possibly cayenne or sage and other spices, mixed with vinegar. (R)

GATES & SONS: Medium consistency, peppery and piquant. Available in both hot and mild versions. (R,S,M)

HARRIS': Robust and tangy with cumin and other seasonings. The sauce is steamed rather than cooked, before it is served on top of meat. (R)

H&M: Spicy-sweet, with a mild aftertaste. (R)

HAYWARD'S: Mild, honey-based and ketchupy, with a touch of cumin. (R,s)

KEEGAN'S: Two kinds of sauce, smoky and spicy, or mild and sweet. (R)

LITTLE JAKE'S: Thick, hearty, sweet and hot, but not too hot. (R,M)

K.C. MASTERPIECE: Black Label is thick and tomatoey with molasses and spices. Red Label is hotter, with a chili powder flavor. There are also mesquite and hickory-flavored barbecue sauces and a No Salt variety. (S,M,N)

MARGARET'S: Sweet and spicy with lemon, pepper and garlic. (R)

MOLLY POTT'S: Ketchup-based, and fired up with cayenne and spices. (R,s)

PAPA LEW & SONS: Mild and sweet with a hint of celery. (R)

OSCAR'S: Tangy and pungent, with a hint of cumin. (R)

RICHARD'S: Incendiary with pepper and paprika with a grainy quality similar to Bryant's but thicker and spicier. (R)

ROSEDALE: Thin and surprisingly potent, with a tingly aftertaste. (R)

SAMMY'S: Mild, with a pleasant aftertaste. (R)

SHERMAN'S: Peppery with garlic, sage, and other spices to make it tart. (Not for sale.)

SMOKE STACK: Piquant, smoky, with a kick to it. (R)

SNEAD'S: Two varieties. One is tomato-based with a pungent aftertaste; the other is a mild, darker sauce, laced with molasses and sweet. (R,M)

STEPHENSON'S: Mellow and slightly spicy. (R)

THREE FRIENDS: Hot, laced with garlic and pepper and a little brown sugar. (Not for sale)

WINSLOW'S: Spicy with jalapeno peppers, garlic and sweetened with molasses. (R,M)

WOLFERMAN'S: Tomato-based, sweet and thick, with a slightly smoky flavor. (Available only at Wolferman's, M)

ZARDA: Tangy with hickory-smoked flavor and molasses. Hot and mild versions available. (R,S,M)

Beef brisket and pork ribs are the two most common cuts for barbecuing. Before you put them on the grill, here are some important things worth remembering.

BRISKET

The whole brisket is a belly muscle of beef which is tough enough to need tenderizing before you cook it. There are two ways to tenderize this unusually tough piece of meat. You can use a wet marinade to help break down the fibers, or cook slowly to allow for the breaking down of fiber.

A whole brisket weighs between five and 12 pounds untrimmed. It has a thick end or "point" and a thin or "flat" end. The brisket is covered with fat on one side and has another large layer of fat which extends inside the point end. The fat acts as a natural baste and adds an excellent taste to the meat as it cooks. Once the meat is done, the fat may be trimmed and discarded.

RIBS

The very choicest ribs for barbecuing are determined by two factors: (1) location of the ribs; (2) the weight and size of the ribs. If you're confused about barbecued pork ribs and the various names used to identify them, and want to know how spareribs differ from loin ribs, country back ribs and baby back ribs, just refer to the drawings below.

ILLUSTRATION (1)

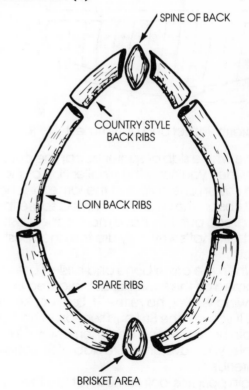

SPINE OF BACK

COUNTRY STYLE BACK RIBS

LOIN BACK RIBS

SPARE RIBS

BRISKET AREA

The three main anatomical rib cuts— country back, loin and sparerib.

ILLUSTRATION (2)

Loin back rib, with all 13 ribs intact. The entire 13 ribs of any rib cut is called a **slab**. When cut in half, it forms a half slab.

ILLUSTRATION (3)

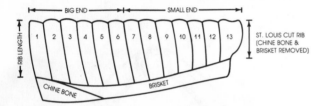

Sparerib, intact and untrimmed.

The whole slab of spareribs can be cut in half. Then you have the smaller ribs, or short end ribs on one half, and the large, or long end ribs on the other. Untrimmed spareribs are great, but they have more bone, gristle and fat. That's why they are the cheapest rib cut.

When the chine bone and brisket are trimmed off the sparerib, as indicated in drawing #3, you have the St. Louis, or Kelso, cut. If you cut the St. Louis section in half, you again have the long and short ends. If left whole, you have an entire slab of St. Louis cut spareribs.

Loin pork ribs look somewhat like the trimmed St. Louis cut, but they are different. Loin ribs are generally the preferred cut and require less trimming because they are meatier.

Weights of Ribs

The weight of the entire slab determines the choicest meatiest ribs, regardless of whether they are loin or spareribs. Since small weight slabs of ribs are usually meatier, they are considered the best and most expensive.

When the whole, untrimmed slabs of either loin or sparerib are weighed, they are grouped and named according to four major weights: whole slabs weighing under two pounds being called "two and under," followed by slabs weighing "three and under," "three to five," and "five pounds and over."

Therefore loin back pork ribs (meatiest cut) two pounds and under (meatiest weight) are the choicest. The country-style back ribs (see drawing #1) are also meaty, but have more bone per pound. St. Louis cut, and spareribs are next in line. Still, if you can afford it, the small loin back ribs are tops for the money.

That's rib talk, translated.

"A small bone is the key to a good rib. More meat than bone. To me that's barbecue."

**Walt Coffey
Longbranch Saloons**

THE PRINCIPLES OF GOOD BARB____

So far we hope you've had fun reading. Now it's time to get out and barbecue, Kansas City-style. Here are some important things to remember before you put that brisket on the grill:

1. SMOKE IT SLOW AND KEEP THE FIRE LOW—Legitimate, native American barbecue, including Kansas City-style barbecue, requires patience and a slow hand. Barbecuing is neither grilling, nor cool smoking and it can't really be done with gas or electric fires, although you can use gas and electric fire-starters to start the process. To barbecue right, you use low heat (175-225 degrees) and smoke from live wood or charcoal fires. Use open-pit methods for lightly smoked meat or closed-pit methods for heavily smoked meat. This way, the meat is both cooked and smoked until well done. (As a rule, barbecue is never served rare, although the rule is broken occasionally for a large whole beef tenderloin.)

The importance of cooking barbecue slowly was brought home when Rich Davis, one of the authors of this book, taught a course in barbecuing in California. Because class time was so limited, he found, to his dismay, that he could not produce the slow-cooked Kansas City-style brisket he intended. Instead the result was flavorful but sadly underdone. What made it worse was that the fire had gone out on the water smoker, without his knowledge.

Fortunately, Joe Rapport, the chef-owner of the cooking school, restarted the fire, avoiding a total disaster and finished the barbecue. (Which probably goes to show that even pros have their dog days.)

It is impossible to barbecue a genuine Kansas City barbecued brisket in less than eight hours. This is the bare minimum. Many a prize-winning brisket will barbecue for 10 to 20 hours. This slow cooking process may require basting to keep the meats moist, which leads to principle number two.

2. USE HIGH HEAT ONLY WHEN GRILLING OR SEARING MEAT. Place the meat directly over a hot fire. Cover the grill and leave the air vents open to allow for oxygen flow to the fire. This will increase the heat. You might consider using liquid marinades to expedite the searing time.

3. DON'T TRIM THE FAT OFF THE BRISKET AND RIBS BEFORE YOU SMOKE IT. In traditional barbecuing it's essential that you leave the fat on the meat during barbecuing so that it will continually moisten and baste the meat. Cook the meat *fat side up* and keep it as far from the fire as possible.

Of course, when the food is done, the fat should be trimmed off before the meat is sliced or the ribs are served. There is almost always a huge hunk of fat lying in and around a whole brisket. You can remove this after the cooking process has been completed and the meat has cooled.

Simply trim the exterior fat by raising the upper layer of the cooked brisket and slicing out the excess. Then slice the remaining meat. There is enough crispness left on the brisket so you'll get both the juicy, well-smoked, well-done interior as well as the crisp exterior.

Fat, the natural moistening agent of these meats, is essential for producing both a flavorful and juicy inside. However, over the hours the fat drips away. For health-conscious people, this is an important factor, since cooking meat this way and trimming the fat actually results in less cholesterol than frying the same cut of meat.

This natural fat-basting principle also applies to open-pit cooking of pork barbecue, common in the southeastern part of the United States. A whole hog, with the skin and fat left on the animal, continually bastes itself to produce a rich flavor. When the meat is chopped, the fat is sectioned out and thrown away.

The perfect barbecued ribs in Kansas City are described as having a touch of char on the end and a darkened, almost crisp coating on part of the outside of the rib. The pinkness that goes through is obviously from the smoking process, not from being underdone. The interior of the rib remains moist if not overly trimmed, even with a crusty outside.

Crust and juice—that's real art. It can be done, but not without adhering to the simple basics of Kansas City barbecue.

4. REMEMBER TRADITIONAL AMERICAN BARBECUED MEATS ARE ALWAYS WELL DONE. Any pinkness results from the slow smoking. There are contemporary barbecuers who will smoke-cook whole beef tenderloin for an hour, leaving the interior medium rare. This might be called *nouvelle barbecue.*

5. DON'T CONFUSE GRILLING WITH BARBECUING. We've alluded to this before. Barbecuing, meaning slow smoke-cooking, is always done with the charcoal or hardwood fire at some distance from the meat. This is difficult to achieve with the round barbecue cookers in which the fire in the center is directly under the food. When using this type of cooker for barbecue, the fire is often banked to one side and the meats placed on the opposite side. It's also essential that the coals be lowered as far as possible from the grill or the grill elevated well above the goals.

Many barbecue aficionados recommend using a water smoker. This is a closed-smoker unit with a pan at the bottom to hold charcoal. Above the charcoal is another pan that contains water and liquid seasoning agents. Above this is the grillwork that holds the meat. This type of smoker, which produces a superior smoke-flavored barbecue, has recently become quite popular.

These units take longer to cook because the temperature at the top meat level is lower and the smoke heavier. The only drawback to this method, according to several barbecue contest winners, is that too much heat under the water pan tends to steam the meat and can eliminate the crusty exterior.

Others insist that the oil drum cooker makes the best barbecue, having no water unit at all. When building the fire and positioning the meat on the grill, don't place the meat directly over the coals, unless it's at a safe distance.

You can also put an aluminum pan of water in the center of a round unit and build the charcoal fire around the edges, then position the meat above the water pan.

The drawing here shows how to barbecue for many hours without burning the meat, leaving the interior moist and delicious.

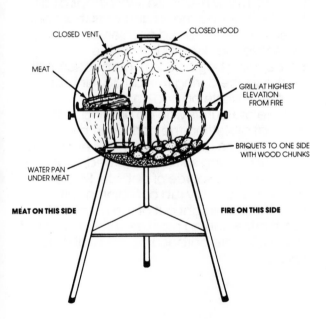

CLOSED VENT

CLOSED HOOD

MEAT

GRILL AT HIGHEST
ELEVATION
FROM FIRE

BRIQUETS TO ONE SIDE
WITH WOOD CHUNKS

WATER PAN
UNDER MEAT

MEAT ON THIS SIDE

FIRE ON THIS SIDE

6. TAKE BOTH WIND AND OUTDOOR TEMPERATURE INTO CONSIDERATION WHEN COOKING BARBECUE. It's simply common sense, yet many a novice forgets to allow for the temperature outdoors when barbecuing.

Barbecuing a brisket in summer with the sun bearing down on the unit will cook foods far more rapidly. It also tends to dry them out since the unit is heated by both the sun and the charcoal.

Barbecuing outdoors in winter (which many Kansas Citians do regularly) eliminates one of these heat sources, so additional charcoal or a longer cooking time has to make up the difference.

Also take into consideration not only the temperature, but also the *degree* of wind. A good barbecue unit is reasonably well-sealed so that it will smoke and slow cook, with a vent providing more or less air to heighten the fire.

There also has to be some inlet of air or the fire will go out. Therefore, on a windy day, the wind will force itself into various crevices and niches that ordinarily wouldn't be producing much exchange of air. As a result, the charcoal will burn hotter and the meat will cook more rapidly.

"The weather makes a lot of difference on how the fire burns and how the temperature stays. One time your ribs might come out in two and a half hours. The next time it might take three hours."
Frank Hipsher
Porky's Pit Barbecue

A cold wind creates a dilemma. The cold *lowers* the heat, and the wind *increases* the flame and heat. By learning the control of the elements and the basics, you'll be able to produce the kind of barbecue you want.

7. <u>LEARN WHEN TO USE SAUCES.</u> Another common error <u>novices make is putting sauce on the barbecue before or during</u> the cooking process.Although most people would not consider cooking asparagus *in* Hollandaise sauce, many see nothing wrong with basting barbecued meats continuously with tomatoey sauces. To barbecue pros, this is sacrilege! <u>Marinate in vinegar-based liquid or dry rub, yes. But marinating in a red table sauce? Definitely not.</u>

This is particularly true for the tomato-based and heavily sweetened barbecue sauces. Both tomato and sugar tend to burn and turn black at reasonably low temperatures so placing barbecue sauce in the oven at the beginning is an error, in our estimation. This principle, however, does not apply to vinegar, wine or seasoned basting liquids.

There is one exception that <u>many Kansas Citians make. They baste the meat during the last 30 to 45 minutes with their favorite barbecue sauce. This seals the meat and produces an excellent aroma and taste.</u>

A few prefer to brush on a tomato-based sauce mixed with honey throughout the cooking process. Some of these honey bastes can heighten flavor and moisture. But this is possible only if the fire is low enough and you prefer a bit of charring on the outside of the meat. Don't forget to check the meat regularly so it doesn't burn.

Barbecue sauces are generally served at the table so people can add them if they prefer. (In Kansas City it's common for restaurants to have a squeeze bottle filled with barbecue sauce.)

"Good barbecue should be slow-cooked, tender and juicy, with a hickory-smoked taste that goes all the way through. To me, the sauce makes all the difference in the world."

Doretha Bryant
Bryant's Barbecue

There is great conflict among professional barbecuers about pre-seasoning and basting. Many never use seasonings at all on their barbecued meats and add them only after the meat is sliced and served. Others use seasoned dry rubs before the barbecuing begins. Some barbecuers paint on the sauce during the last 30 minutes, and still others baste off and on.

There are purists who do nothing to the meat at all, letting the barbecue process itself produce all the flavor they'll ever need.

As far as using salt is concerned, that is another great source of debate. Some swear that any dry rub containing salt will suck the juices right out of the meat. Yet some prizewinning pros use a sugar and salt mixture before barbecuing and get great results.

> **"You have to be willing to take a risk. Creative cooks keep trying different things. Sure, you might lose a few dollars worth of meat, but you could also wind up with a real prize-winner.**
> **Paul Kirk**
> **Molly Potts Chops and Chicken**

8. MAKE THE BEST USE OF WOOD. Select your woods based on availability, cost and flavor. Mesquite produces the hottest fire. Hickory is most readily available and produces a heavy smoke flavor. Fruit wood has a mellow taste. Never use pine or other resinous soft woods.

When grilling add water-soaked *chips* directly to the coals (see section on woods in "The Mastery of Kansas City Barbecue.") Place a pan of water over the fire top to add moisture and maximize tenderizing. To provide continuous moisture, put the water pan over the fire underneath, and opposite the meat on the grill.

> **"The wood is kind of like a spice. It enhances the flavor and it's just as important as the sauce."**
> **Frank Hipsher**
> **Porky's Pit Barbecue**

Many barbecuers also use the "dry" method of smoking ribs, preferring to keep them crusted with blackened tips, and don't use the water pan at all.

Wood chips and sawdust are fine for grilling; chunks are best for barbecuing. The longer the wood soaks, the better the smoke. Small chips should sit in water at least 30 minutes; big chunks of wood, at least 10 to 12 hours before cooking.

9. HOW TO USE CHARCOAL BRIQUETS FOR BEST RESULTS. Allow the charcoal to ash down. A small charcoal fire for covered smoke cooking provides an excellent heat source as well as a means of producing smoke from the wood. Heat doesn't escape as it does with open barbecuing, and a little fuel goes a long way.

You can start with between 12 and 25 briquets in your kettle. This should last from one to two hours. Add more briquets as needed. Serious barbecuers use cookers that have the advantage of fireboxes that provide for easy loading of additional charcoal and wood. (See section on grills in "The Mastery of Kansas City Barbecue.")

10. ALWAYS BRING MEAT TO ROOM TEMPERATURE BEFORE COOKING. This gives the best results.

> **"Don't put cold meat on the grill. That's bad. Take it out of the refrigerator, wash it down, rub it good with spices and let it sit around for a while until it comes to room temperature. Then cook it slow. That's good."**
> **Bruce "Doc" Daniel**
> **"Doc" Daniel's Barbecue Sauce**

PUTTING IT ALL TOGETHER

HOW TO FIX BARBECUED RIBS KANSAS CITY-STYLE

Now that we've reviewed the basics from woods to seasonings, this simple step-by-step method for preparing barbecued ribs should tie it all together. This is just one of the dozens of variations of how to barbecue ribs the way Kansas Citians do. (For more ways to fix ribs, see the recipe section).

1. Place a chimney firestarter in your barbecue unit.

2. Place crushed newspaper in the bottom section and put 12-15 charcoal briquets in the top part of the chimney. (Use 100 percent hardwood charcoal, if possible, for the best results). Light the newspapers in the lower section.

3. Take three whole slabs of loin back pork ribs, preferably two pounds and under. Season with a dry rub or coat ribs on all sides lightly with prepared mustard. Then sprinkle generously with paprika, and dark brown sugar, and some cracked black pepper if you want spicy ribs.

4. Add two pre-moistened hickory chunks when the coals are red.

5. Do not spread the charcoal out as for grilling. Place ribs fat side up in smoker, away from the fire and close the lid, leaving the damper barely open. Do not open the lid except to add more briquets and wood chunks. You won't need a heavy smoke if you're planning to barbecue for several hours. Some smoke should be seeping from the edges of the smoker, or from the barely opened damper at all times.

6. Don't allow the fire to flare. Occasionally when you open the lid to add briquets, it may flame up. This usually subsides when the lid is closed tightly, but a spray of water away from the food will put out the flame. Remember that such a fire is much too hot for barbecuing.

7. Smoke-cook at 200 degrees for four to six hours. Ribs can be stacked and rotated to maintain juices for self-basting. They do not need turning unless the fire has gotten too hot and has overbrowned a side.

8. Turn the ribs during the last 30 minutes (with the fat side down), baste generously with barbecue sauce and let smoke. Use about one cup of sauce per slab.

9. Let cool down enough to handle and serve with additional barbecue sauce on the side.

INDOOR METHOD

If you can't get outdoors for real barbecue, here's a reasonable facsimile that produces excellent results. (Also see indoor ways to fix ribs in the recipe section.)

1. Parboil ribs (optional) or cook them as they are.

2. Coat ribs with liquid hickory smoke (2 tablespoons per slab). Cover ribs with the same mustard/dry rub mentioned in the outdoor method.

3. Preheat oven to 400 degrees. Place ribs on a rack in a pan and cook for 15 minutes. Reduce the heat to 250 degrees and cook another two hours.

4. Baste with your favorite barbecue sauce and cook an additional 30 minutes.

THE RECIPES

In this section you'll find just a sampling of what Kansas City has to offer in the way of barbecue—from First Prize-winning recipes for beef, pork, poultry, and seafood, to outstanding Kansas City barbecue dishes served at the recent Presidential Inaugural Celebration.

Most of the recipes feature traditional outdoor barbecue. However there are a few indoor "mock" barbecue dishes as well as a couple of quick cheaters on the grill for those who don't have the time or patience to indulge in the real thing.

Included here are mouth-watering selections such as barbecued venison ribs and marinated beef briskets, as well as honey-basted pork loin and hickory-smoked leg of lamb with natural rosemary sauce.

Please note that brand-named products are included only because individual contributors specified these products as necessary flavoring agents for their recipes.

BARBECUED BEEF

DAVE HALSEY'S BLUE RIBBON BEEF BRISKET

**One 5-pound brisket, cut in half
teriyaki sauce (enough to cover
   meat)
Morton's Nature's Seasons to taste
1 can beer
K.C. Masterpiece barbecue sauce
   (any label)**

Marinate the brisket overnight in a mixture of teriyaki sauce and Morton's seasonings. Put your coals on and let heat for 45 minutes. (Halsey uses a Weber kettle and places the meat in the center of the grill with charcoal on either side). Stack the briskets one on top of the other and leave in this position for 10 minutes with the lid closed at 300 degrees. Rotate the meat, putting the top half on the bottom and cooking it 10 minutes more. Repeat the process on the other side of each piece of meat. (This sealing procedure takes around 40 minutes). Continue to rotate the meat every 20 minutes at 225 degrees for several hours, basting with beer to keep moist on the outside. Baste with barbecue sauce an additional 30 minutes, rotating the meat every five minutes to avoid burning. Serves eight.

RICH DAVIS' INDOOR BARBECUED MARINATED BEEF BRISKET

5-8 pound brisket
1/4 cup liquid smoke
1/4 cup Worcestershire sauce
1/3 cup Italian salad dressing
1/4 cup liquid B-V (or other liquid
          beef concentrate)
1 tablespoon finely minced garlic
19-oz. bottle K.C. Masterpiece
     barbecue sauce—red label

First day: Place brisket on a large sheet of foil in large baking dish. Mix all ingredients with one cup K.C. Masterpiece and pour over brisket. Let it sit for 15 minutes. Then seal foil to cover meat completely. Place in refrigerator to marinate overnight.

Second day: Do not uncover. Bake in a 300 degree oven for four hours. Cool. Place in refrigerator overnight.

Third day: Remove meat and discard fat and foil. Slice brisket across the grain with a sharp knife and pour remaining K.C. Masterpiece over meat. Reheat at 350 degrees for 30 minutes. Serve a bowl of K.C. Masterpiece for additional sauce. Serves eight.

RICH DAVIS' BARBECUED WHOLE TENDERLOIN

3 large pork tenderloins (or one whole trimmed beef tenderloin) —room temperature

(marinade)
1 cup soy sauce
1/3 cup oriental sesame oil
3 large cloves garlic, minced
1 tablespoon ground ginger
1 teaspoon MSG (optional)

(sauce)
one 19-oz. bottle K.C. Masterpiece barbecue sauce (any label)
1/3 cup soy sauce
1/4 cup oriental sesame oil
1 large garlic clove, finely minced

Marinate tenderloins overnight in the refrigerator in marinade of soy sauce, sesame oil, garlic, ginger and monosodium glutamate. Place tenderloins on charcoal grill (with moistened hickory chips to smoke) over low fire, turning every 15 minutes and basting with marinade. Barbecue with lid closed to smoke, approximately 1½ hours for pork (or until beef is done to preferred rareness).

Blend K.C. Masterpiece with soy sauce, sesame oil and garlic for sauce. Stir well. Serve heated sauce at the table with meat. Serves eight.

Note: For indoor barbecuing, rub tenderloins generously with K.C. Masterpiece liquid hickory or mesquite smoke, marinate overnight in above mixture, then cook in 300 degree preheated oven, following basting directions above to desired doneness.

This recipe won first prize at the Colorado Beef Grower's Contest and first prize at the American Royal Barbecue Contest in 1980 using whole pork tenderloin.

BETTY GOSS' BEEF TENDERLOIN

5-7 pounds beef tenderloin whole, trimmed
1 stick melted butter
1 jar barbecue sauce
2 teaspoons garlic salt
aluminum foil
hickory chips (presoaked in water for 30 minutes)

Marinate the tenderloin overnight in the mixture of butter, barbecue sauce and garlic salt. Remove the tenderloin, saving the marinade. Grill the tenderloin, 15 minutes each side on outdoor grill, over a hot fire and hickory chips. Remove the tenderloin and place on foil wrap in pan. Pour remaining marinade over the tenderloin, fold the foil over and seal it tight. Cook one hour at 300 degrees. Cook less time if you want it rarer. Use a meat thermometer for accurate cooking temperature, inserting the thermometer into the meat, and wrapping foil tightly around it. Serves six to eight.

BOB BURROWS

An award-winning illustrator and consulting art director, Bob Burrows took time out from his busy schedule to design this book. By his own admission, his hectic lifestyle often necessitates cooking short-cuts. The following recipe is, according to the artist, a real cheater since you can turn out nearly authentic barbecue in a short amount of time.

As Burrows points out, the recipe is part of the "Yuppie" life he once embraced years ago when he wore three-piece suits and shined his shoes twice a day. The resulting effort is suitable for a romantic dinner for two.

"Pick somebody you really like, 'cause the damn thing costs a lot to make," says Burrows.

BOB BURROWS BOUR·BON·CUE

1 cup genuine Kentucky
   sour mash straight bourbon
1/2 cup liquid brown sugar
1/2 stick butter
barbecue sauce
one 2-pound steak, 1 1/2 inches
   thick

Mix bourbon and liquid brown sugar in a Pyrex dish large enough to hold the steak. Let steak marinate in mixture for two hours in the refrigerator.

Remove steak, turn it over and marinate on other side for an additional two hours. When time is up, remove steak and drain it. (According to Burrows, it is supposed to look "gray and scuzzy" at this point).

Fire up the grill and get it real hot. Prior to putting the steak on to cook Burrows suggests that you "nuke" the meat in a microwave for two minutes each side in order to achieve maximum showmanship on the grill.

Take what's left of marinade, add melted butter and your favorite red barbecue sauce until you have a barbecue sauce of loose consistency. Dip steak into mixture on both sides.

*NOTE: The steak, coated with alcohol and brown sugar, will flame on the grill. Be sure to use a long-handled fork for turning and wear gloves. The barbecue sauce will be sucked right into the bourbon-laced meat, and you get a piece of meat that is burned black on the outside and stays blood rare on the inside.

When the steak is all crusty, remove it and serve with tart salad and baked potato. Serves two.

This is a token "cheater" in the book for people who hate to take the time to barbecue.

CHARLES BARSOTTI

Nationally known cartoonist, Charles Barsotti, is a native Texan who lives in Kansas City for reasons even he doesn't understand. When not hard at work drawing cartoons for "USA Today," "The New Yorker," and "Texas Monthly" he barbecues up a storm with recipes he claims are Texas imports.

According to Barsotti, the secret of good backyard barbecue is in the "mucking about."

"Never wear a funny apron and always muck about with panache," he says. "You can get panache in the spice section of any good market."

His irreverent cartoon is seen below. However, we feel Barsotti's sense of direction is misguided. Perhaps Lockhart, Texas, folks should head north on I-35 for a taste of Kansas City barbecue instead!

BARSOTTI'S FAJITAS-KANSAS CITY-STYLE

3 pound skirt steak or flank steak
16 oz. bottle of Italian dressing
Flour tortillas
Salsa Alicia (see recipe below)

Marinate meat in Italian dressing for around four hours. Drain. Cook over mesquite chips for 20 minutes on a hot fire until the meat reaches preferred doneness. Cut meat into small strips. Smother with Salsa Alicia, wrap in warm flour tortillas and serve.

SALSA ALICIA

3 strips bacon cut into small pieces
1/2 cup chopped onion
1/2 cup chopped green pepper
16 oz. can whole tomatoes
1 tsp. salt
2 or 3 chopped jalapeno peppers

Fry bacon. Saute onion and green peppers, add tomatoes, salt and jalapeno peppers. Simmer together on low fire 20 minutes until done. Serve over meat and tortillas. Serves six.

BARBECUED GAME

JOHN F. (BUFFALO) GATTENBY

John F. Gattenby, who claims he's as big as a "buffalo," received his unusual nickname from his fellow workers. He built his own meat smoker (see homemade smokers) using an old refrigerator. He uses hickory, apple, wild cherry and hackberry woods to give his meat an unusual flavor.

"I prepare what I cook like I was baking it," says Gattenby. "I season it to taste, but don't coat it with butter or oil because it prevents the smoke from entering the meat."

To determine when the meat is done, Gattenby uses a meat thermometer on turkey and deer—although it's hard to find the right place on smaller game—the recipe for which you'll find right here.

BUFFALO'S BARBECUED SQUIRREL

hickory, cherry and apple wood chips
1 squirrel or rabbit, dressed, washed and patted dry
1 cup Heinz 57 sauce
1 cup honey

Soak mixture of hickory, cherry and apple woods in a bucket all night and use when you smoke the meat. Prepare fresh meat immediately. Cook at 200 degrees in an aluminum tray and baste continually with juices until the meat is tender (at least 1-2 hours). Glaze with a mixture of Heinz 57 and honey 20 minutes before you take the meat off the grill. Serves one to two.

CAROLYN WELLS

In that mysterious, macho sport of barbecue, few women have dared enter the male domain of competition. But Carolyn Wells is an exception. The Executive Vice President of Wicker's Barbecue Products, Wells claims she can pit her ribs against anybody's and has the trophies to prove it.

She enjoys the legend that surrounds her company's product. The unique wet marinade has been a favorite of Southeast Missourians ever since the late Peck Wicker began making the secret concoction over an earthen pit in his back yard in Hornersville, Mo., in 1940. Eventually author and columnist, Craig Claiborne, got wind of Wicker, wrote him up and a legend was born. Today the vinegar-based sauce, which contains no sugar or tomatoes, is a Southern tradition that is catching on around the country.

CAROLYN WELLS' VENISON RIBS

side of venison ribs
1/2 cup salad oil
1/4 cup vinegar
1/4 cup onion, chopped
1 teaspoon salt
2 teaspoons Worcestershire sauce
1 quart bottle Lambrusco
1 bottle Wicker's

Combine all ingredients, place ribs in covered pan and marinate for four days in refrigerator. Turn twice a day. Drain marinade. Place ribs on grill and baste with Wicker's four hours over low heat (200 degrees). Enjoy with corn on the cob and squash casserole. Serves three to four.

DAVE HALSEY'S PRIZE-WINNING BARBECUED VENISON

one 3 pound venison roast
3/4 cup wine vinegar
3/4 cup cooking oil
3/4 cup ketchup
3 tablespoons Worcestershire
**   sauce**
1 1/2 tablespoons garlic salt
1 1/2 teaspoons dry mustard
sprinkle of pepper
Morton's Nature's Seasons to taste
K.C. Masterpiece barbecue sauce
**   (any label)**

Season meat with Morton's seasoning and mix the ingredients above into a marinade. Cover the roast with the marinade and let it sit overnight to tenderize. Remove roast, saving leftover marinade. Put on your coals and let them cook down 45 minutes. (Halsey uses a Weber Grill and places the meat in the center of the grill with charcoal on either side). To seal meat put it on hot grill (with lid on) for the first 30 minutes, turning every five minutes to make sure it doesn't dry out. Let cook one and a half hours more at 225 degrees, turning every 15 to 20 minutes and basting occasionally with leftover marinade. Cook an additional 30 minutes, basting frequently with K.C. Masterpiece sauce, continuing to turn the meat every five minutes so it doesn't burn. Serves four to six.

BARBECUED LAMB

KEN DUNN
Chef, American Restaurant

The American Restaurant's chef, Ken Dunn, has truly American roots, having been raised and educated in the Midwest.

Chef Dunn attended Iowa State University, majoring in Hotel and Restaurant Management. His participation in the American Culinary Federation shows across the nation has earned three bronze medals, one silver medal and a special judges award for the most original piece of show.

Included here is Chef Dunn's unusual version of K.C.-style barbecue served upon request at the American Restaurant.

AMERICAN RESTAURANT'S BARBECUED LEG OF LAMB WITH NATURAL ROSEMARY SAUCE

10 pounds whole bone-in leg of lamb
1 tablespoon salt
1 tablespoon freshly ground black pepper
4 cloves freshly minced garlic
2 teaspoons paprika
3/4 cup freshly chopped rosemary
8 pounds charcoal
3 pounds apple wood chips
3 pounds cherry wood chips
3 pounds mesquite wood chips
3 bottles beer
1 bottle white wine

Prepare the leg of lamb by rubbing it with herbs and seasonings, making sure they are evenly distributed. Place wood chips in a large basin and soak in cool water for one hour. Place beer and wine in a metal cake pan. Light charcoal and let burn until coals are red. Distribute several handfuls of mixed wood chips on top of the coals. Set the pan of beer and wine mixture on top of chips and replace the grate on grill.

Place leg of lamb on grate and cover tightly with either the grill lid or heavy duty aluminum foil so that a minimum amount of smoke escapes. Add two handfuls of wood chips every 20 minutes or so to keep the smoke going. Cook until the internal temperature of the leg of lamb is 125 degrees, or lamb reaches desired doneness (approximately three hours, depending on heat of coals). Serve sliced thin with Natural Rosemary Sauce. Serves eight to 10.

NATURAL ROSEMARY BARBECUE SAUCE
(See next page)

NATURAL ROSEMARY BARBECUE SAUCE

**20 pounds lamb shank bones,
    split and roasted dark brown**
**3 yellow onions, peeled and
    coarsely chopped**
**6 carrots, peeled and coarsely
    chopped**
1/2 bunch celery, coarsely chopped
1 1/2 cups fresh rosemary, chopped
1 1/2 cloves garlic, crushed
10 bay leaves
1/4 cup fresh thyme, chopped
2 1/2 cups Hunt's chili sauce
2 cups red currant jelly
3 yellow banana peppers
1/2 cup red wine, optional
2 tablespoons cornstarch, optional

Have butcher select good fresh shank bones and have them split or cut on the bandsaw. Place bones into heavy roasting pan and brown at 425 degrees until dark, golden brown. Place bones in heavy stock pot that holds at least two gallons. Set to one side. In the same pan that the bones were roasted, place onions, carrots and celery. Put in oven at 425 degrees and cook until very brown, stirring every 10 minutes. When vegetables are brown, place them in the stock pot with the bones. Cover with cold water and add all herbs and seasonings.

Put pot on high heat on range and bring to a boil. Turn the heat back and simmer for six hours or more. (The longer it cooks, the better the flavor). Strain out bones and vegetables and add current jelly, chili sauce and banana peppers to the stock. Simmer stock over low heat for one hour. Sauce should be thickened naturally by this time, but the red wine may be mixed with two tablespoons of cornstarch and added (mix thoroughly and cook a few minutes longer). Serves eight to 10.

FRED WOLFERMAN'S BARBECUED LAMB RIBLETS APPETIZER

lamb riblets (3-4 riblets per person, trimmed from rack of lamb)
Wolferman's Barbecue Sauce

Spread enough barbecue sauce to cover the riblets. Bake at 350 degrees for 45 minutes and serve.

FRED WOLFERMAN

The owner of Wolferman's gourmet grocery store in Fairway, Kansas, Fred Wolferman has created his own brand of barbecue sauce which won "Best in the U.S.A." honors at the First Annual Diddy Wa Diddy Barbecue Sauce Tasting in Olathe, Kansas. His recipe for barbecued lamb riblets can be served as an appetizer and, according to Fred, they are "simple, unusual, and delicious." Served with Wolferman's famous English muffins on the side and you've got a real "made in Kansas City" treat in store.

BARBECUED POULTRY

DAVE "BUFFALO" HALSEY

Dave "Buffalo" Halsey started barbecuing for friends back in Butler, Mo. seven years ago. They convinced him to enter the first American Royal Barbecue contest and he enjoyed competing. Since then he's been cooking up a storm, winning nine blue ribbons and taking first place in the categories of pork, ribs, beef, poultry and lamb (see Halsey's recipes for pork shoulder, pork ribs, brisket and venison). Halsey's never-fail methods utilize a Weber kettle, with the meat placed in the center of the grill with charcoal on either side. In addition, Halsey always lets the coals heat 45 minutes until they ash over.

BARBECUED GIZZARDS

2-3 lb. box of chicken gizzards
Morton's Nature's Seasons to taste
K.C. Masterpiece barbecue sauce
(your choice of labels)

Season gizzards with Morton's seasoning. Cook the gizzards at the same time you cook the chicken, filling in the spaces between the pieces of chicken on the grill with gizzards and cooking them over a low fire (200-225 degrees) until tender. Remove gizzards from fire and let soak in a pan of barbecue sauce. These are guaranteed to melt in your mouth! Serves four to six.

DAVE HALSEY'S BLUE RIBBON BARBECUED CHICKEN

4-6 chicken quarters (less
handling and turning)
Morton's Nature's Seasons to taste
K.C. Masterpiece barbecue sauce
(your choice of labels)

Put on your coals and let them heat up 45 minutes. Season chicken to taste with Morton's seasonings. Cover grill with a single layer of chicken quarters and let chicken sear five to seven minutes on each side at 300 degrees. Let fire cool down to 225 degrees and cook one and a half hours, turning chicken every 15 minutes. Cook chicken an additional 20 minutes, basting with barbecue sauce and turning the chicken every five minutes so it doesn't burn. Serves four to six.

PHIL GUTTENDORF
Executive Chef, Peppercorn Duck Club, Hyatt Regency Hotel

Phil Guttendorf graduated from the Culinary Institute of America in 1969 with honors. He joined Hyatt as Executive Sous Chef for the Hyatt hotel in Lexington and was promoted to Executive Chef for the Hyatt Regency, Kansas City.

Can a gourmet chef prepare barbecue Kansas City-style? You bet. As a matter of fact, Guttendorf's recipe was especially created for the American Royal barbecue contest and is now served at the Kansas City-based Hyatt Regency upon request.

HYATT REGENCY PEPPERCORN DUCK CLUB SMOKED DUCK

4 to 4 1/2 pound duckling
1 teaspoon each of rosemary,
**   fennel, anise, garlic powder,**
**   white pepper, and paprika**
1/2 cup salt
hickory chips

Trim duck, remove tail, neck flap, wings after the first joint, and knuckles on the legs. Add seasonings to salt and mix well. Rub seasonings all over outside of duck and put one tablespoon of the mixture inside the duck.

Soak hickory chips in water at least 30 minutes and sprinkle on the coals. The chips will smoulder and impart an excellent taste to the duck, which turns a natural golden red.

Smoke the duck on a banked fire away from the flame for 2 1/2 hours at 200-225 degrees. You'll know when it's done by pushing on the leg. If it moves freely, it's finished. Or when the internal temperature on the thigh reaches 160 to 165 degrees, it's done. Serves two to four.

BRUCE "DOC" DANIEL

All true barbecue "believers" started with an individual who inspired them. Doc Daniel's inspiration came from a friend's father whose dictums of "smoke it slow" and "pepper is the key to good barbecue" still ring true.

Today his homemade "Doc" Daniel's Barbecue sauce is sold in stores and gift catalogues.

BRUCE "DOC" DANIEL'S SMOKED TURKEY

one whole turkey
cooking oil
pepper
hickory chips

Rub bird with cooking oil and pepper including body cavity. Place in shallow pan above indirect charcoal hickory fire. (Use hickory chips that have been soaked in water overnight to create lots of thick, wet smoke). Bring heat in smoker up to 200 degrees and maintain a steady temperature throughout the cooking process. Baste the bird every hour with cooking oil.

Cook for 45 to 60 minutes per pound. Remove bird from pan and place directly on rack for the final two hours of smoking. Serve with "Doc" Daniel's Barbecue Sauce on the side.

DICK MAIS' KANSAS STATE CHAMPIONSHIP CORNISH GAME HEN

4 Cornish game hens
2 cups orange juice
3 tablespoons Cointreau
1/2 stick butter
large bore needle and syringe
paprika
1 cup honey

Mix orange juice, Cointreau and butter over low heat until well blended. Using syringe, inject mixture into each side of the breast and thighs of each bird. Add honey to remaining mixture and use as baste.

Smoke four to six hours on very low grill over mesquite and pecan woods. One-half hour before completion, sprinkle with paprika. Serves four.

BARBECUED PORK

LINDSAY SHANNON

One of the inspirations for this book, Lindsay Shannon has been eating barbecue all his life. That's because this type of food goes well with the jazz and blues that Lindsay loves as much as he does burnt ends. One of the founders of the Kansas City Blues Society, and a member of the advisory board of the Kansas City Jazz Commission, Lindsay produces a radio program called "The Many Phases of the Blues" on KCUR-FM radio which airs Saturday afternoons at 4 p.m. and features blues, R&B, jazz and soul music.

"Blues and barbecue just seem to fit together naturally," says Shannon. According to Shannon, one of the most important ingredients during the smoking process is the kind of music you listen to while cooking. "I'm sure that in Texas, country music is all right for barbecue," he says. "But in Kansas City, blues or jazz blends much better with the smoke.

"Barbecue Bob (Robert Hicks) is a good place to start. Bob recorded his 12-string guitar sound between 1927 and 1930. For a jazzier sound, Sam Price's album 'Rib Joint' cooks right along."

Of course, if you're smoking ribs on a Saturday afternoon, you can listen to The Many Phases of the Blues and catch host Lindsay Shannon playing any one of the following on request: Magic Slim's "TV Dinner Blues"; Albert Collins' "Don't Go Reaching Across My Plate"; Little Milton's "Grits Ain't Groceries"; or Jimmy Smith's "Home Cooking."

LINDSAY SHANNON'S COUNTRY STYLE RIBS

2 slabs of country-style pork ribs
black pepper
hickory chips
barbecue sauce

Separate ribs if necessary and put into large pot of boiling water five minutes. The quick boil breaks down the tough parts of the meat and you won't lose the flavor. Sprinkle ribs with black pepper and let sit at room temperature 30 minutes. Soak your hickory chips in water that same amount of time. Add hickory chips to fire. Place ribs in smoker at opposite end away from fire. Keep lid down and slow cook around 2 1/2 to 3 hours at 200-225 degrees. After they have smoked, put directly over a low fire for a few minutes on each side to give the outside of the meat the right flavor.

Apply a coat of your favorite barbecue sauce just before you take them off the grill. Most of the time Shannon uses a spicy hot sauce from Harris' Barbecue at 24th and Brooklyn (see restaurant section). Serve ribs with a bowl of sauce, your favorite bread, fresh vegetables and Avery Island Potato Pancakes (see Shannon's recipe in the "Unusual Accompaniments" section). Serves four to six.

STEVE STEPHENSON

Steve Stephenson, owner of Steve Stephenson's Apple Tree Inn, uses a smoker to barbecue pork ribs at home. He cautions backyard barbecuers to use plenty of hickory wood and lots of smoke to get the best flavor. "Be sure you have a cover on the top of your grill," he says. "You want the smoke to go completely through the ribs." According to Stephenson, you'll know the ribs are ready if, after you cook them, they pull apart easily. If there is any pressure, they need more smoking.

STEVE STEPHENSON'S BARBECUED RIBS

1 cup salt
1 cup all-purpose seasoning
1 cup monosodium glutamate or
     Accent (optional)
1 cup paprika
5-6 slabs pork spareribs

Let the coals run to almost white before you begin cooking the ribs. Take a big plate and mix seasonings together. Take ribs and, starting at one end, cut each one almost to the top. Lay them on one side of the mixture in the plate. Cover with the mixture and press as much into the ribs as you can. Flip them, cover and press mixture into the other side. Lay ribs in smoker or grill. Let cook 15 minutes on one side. Turn them over for 15 minutes on the other side. Continue to flip each side again every 15 minutes. Cook until the ribs pull apart easily— around 2 1/2 hours at 225 degrees. Serves 10 to 14.

STEVE STEPHENSON'S BARBECUE SAUCE

two 14-oz. bottles ketchup
3 tablespoons horseradish
3 tablespoons salad mustard
     (hotter than regular mustard)
2 tablespoons Worcestershire
     sauce
1 tablespoon lemon juice
1 teaspoon celery seed
1/4 teaspoon onion salt
1/4 teaspoon cayenne pepper
1/4 teaspoon liquid smoke
1/4 teaspoon garlic juice

Blend together all ingredients and refrigerate in a covered glass jar. Heat and serve with meat.

SIMPSON AND DAVIS' CHAMPIONSHIP BARBECUED SPARERIBS

These prize-winning barbecue enthusiasts (see their recipe for sausage) offer yet another way to make barbecued spareribs.

**1 slab spareribs
liquid smoke
garlic salt
celery salt
pepper
1 can of beer (for cooking)
barbecue sauce**

Take spareribs and pull membrane from the top of ribs and the fatty meat portion. This takes some practice, but you should be able to grasp one corner of the meat using needle nose pliers and pull it off in one shot.

Take the skimmed ribs and lightly sprinkle liquid smoke on both sides and rub in by hand. Lightly sprinkle other ingredients over both sides. Place on smoker or pit using indirect heat and cook for around 2 1/2 hours or until bone is exposed about 1/2 inch on the end. Baste with your favorite sauce for the last 30 minutes.

Remember to turn ribs every 45 minutes and keep them moist by dabbing beer on them now and then. The more moisture, the better the ribs. Serves two or three.

DAVE HALSEY'S BLUE RIBBON B...
COUNTRY B...

2 slabs country back ribs
teriyaki sauce, enough to cover
    ribs
Morton's Nature's Seasons to taste
1 can beer
K.C. Masterpiece barbecue sauce
    (any label)

(Marinate:)
  50% Teriyaki & 50% Beer

Do not trim fat from ribs, or p... Marinate with a mixture of teriy... and Morton's Nature's Seasons a... overnight if possible. Let coals ash... around 45 minutes (Halsey uses a W... kettle and places the meat in the center of the grill with charcoal on either side). Stack the ribs, one on top of the other. Leave in this position for around 10 minutes, with the lid closed, at 300 degrees. Rotate the stack, putting top slab on bottom and cooking meat 10 minutes more. Repeat the process on the other side of each slab of ribs. (This takes around 40 minutes in all). Keep rotating the ribs, occasionally basting with beer to keep ribs moist on the outside and turning the fire down to 225 degrees. Turn every 20 to 30 minutes for around two hours. Baste with barbecue sauce for another hour, continuing to rotate the ribs and letting the fire die out naturally. Serves four to six.

1/1/87   Followed the above, but added can of beer to marinade (24 hrs) Pat & Darrell: Great! 5 hrs Build fire one side only!

6/30/91   Same as above: Eric & David:

6/14/96   Same as above: Father's Day; Dick, Helen, Jody, David, & Eric (Laid out Flat, Fire Both sides, Meat side up, Shift every 15 min, 1st hr. 20 min Last 1 1/2 hrs) (fill drip pan with water - 1/2")

4/9/00   Same as above & added Garlic Salt, & Pepper

**whole slabs of loin baby back
   pork ribs
prepared yellow mustard
dark brown sugar
ground black pepper
Hungarian paprika
K.C. Masterpiece black label
   barbecue sauce
salt**

Lightly rub prepared mustard all over ribs. Sprinkle lightly with black pepper (not salt) on both sides. Sprinkle *generously* with paprika on both sides.

Crumble dark brown sugar on both sides of ribs. Press into meat. Place ribs on rack, fat side up, away from charcoal fire with water soaked hickory chunks smoking. Do not grill or place directly over fire, since ribs must smoke for four to five hours (at 200-225 degrees). Check fire occasionally to prevent ribs from turning black. No need to turn ribs during cooking.

The last 30-45 minutes, salt ribs. Then coat top side of ribs generously with K.C. Masterpiece Barbecue Sauce of your choice. Serve when cooled to handle. Also delicious cold the next day.
Serves six.

DAVE HALSEY'S BLUE RIBBON BARBECUED PORK SHOULDER

3-5 pounds pork shoulder with the bone left in
teriyaki sauce
Morton's Nature's Seasons to taste
K.C. Masterpiece (any label)

Marinate meat in a mixture of teriyaki sauce and Morton's seasoning overnight if possible. Let coals ash down 45 minutes (Halsey uses a Weber kettle and places meat in the center of grill with charcoal on either side.) Seal the roast by turning it every 10 minutes at 300 degrees (lid closed) until all exposed sides are seared. Let the fire cool down to 225 degrees and continue turning meat every 20 to 30 minutes, basting occasionally with beer for around two and a half hours. Baste an additional 30 minutes with barbecue sauce, turning meat every five minutes so it doesn't burn.

DICK MAIS

Dick Mais can't recall a period of time since he was 12 that he didn't sample barbecue at least once a week. If he's learned anything in the last 20 years of outdoor cooking, it's that the key ingredient of barbecue is patience and tender loving care. At the urge of family and friends he began participating in regional barbecue contests and has won over 25 awards so far.

Currently involved in marketing mesquite charcoal and various wood products for barbecuing, Mais has plenty to say on the subject of barbecue.

"There are some barbecue pros who hang the meat up rotisserie-style to smoke. Hanging meat cooks slowly, but the juice drops down and falls into the grease catcher. It has a tendency to dry out this way. I cook the meat with the fat side up, laying down. The juice cooks down through the meat and it doesn't dry out. I continually rotate the slabs. When one cooks up on the bottom, I move it to the top to keep the cycle going."

Mais turns up the heat the last half hour of cooking. Where he might cook at 175 degrees for a long time, he'll fire up the grill as high as 250 degrees, open up the vents and allow more oxygen. This technique allows him to cook pork loins—a usually difficult meat to prepare.

"Loins cook very quickly, because there is little fat on them. Just remember to rotate the meat and stack it on a slow grill."

DICK MAIS' PRIZE-WINNING HONEY-SMOKED PORK LOIN

one 3-6 pound Canadian pork loin
1 1/2 cups honey
1/2 cup prepared mustard, such
as Rooker's (a Kansas City-
based company)
dry barbecue spice rub
large bore needle and syringe

Heat the honey until it's the consistency of water, but don't boil. Use the needle and syringe and inject the pork loin with honey in at least four different sites. Cover the loin with prepared mustard and a dry rub. Wrap the loin in foil and let it marinate in refrigerator for at least six hours.

Remove loin and allow it to reach room temperature. It is preferable to smoke the meat at 175 degrees for 12 hours. However, if your oven temperature is hotter, keep the heat as low as possible and smoke for six to eight hours. If you like a red sauce, then use your favorite brand to glaze the loin the last half hour.

Note: Dick Mais recommends smoking the meat over a combination of hickory and mesquite. He also believes that the finest way to enjoy the pork loin is with a Southern-style mustard-based sauce or one that contains such important spices as apple cider vinegar, onions, soy sauce, sugar and blended peppers. Serves six to 12.

AL BOHNERT

Al Bohnert, owner of Bohnert Construction, leads a barbecue team called "Chef Jacques Strappe and His Supporters." They started out as a church group bound and determined to change from charbroiling hamburgers on a grill to something more exciting.

"It took us at least four pigs, but we finally got it right," admits Bohnert. "The first one was raw, the second one burned up, the third one was 'wrong because,' and the fourth one came out right."

Bohnert says that he cooks a whole pig slow: "You can't rush it." He buys his porker at a good meat market and orders up at least a 56-pounder that's been butchered and cleaned. It takes between eight and 10 hours to barbecue the pig, and the result feeds up to 90 people—if they don't make hogs of themselves!

As for the barbecue sauce, Bohnert says: "Make sure it's sweet."

AL BOHNERT'S ROAST PIG

**1 pig—90 pounds maximum
dressed weight
1/2 gallon white vinegar
1 ounce cracked red pepper
barbecue sauce
charcoal
charcoal lighter**

Twenty-four hours before cooking, mix vinegar and pepper. Pig should be whole, clean and dressed, with the skin on. Before placing pig on grill, split the breast bone and approximately the first four ribs and the hip bone so the pig will lay flat on the grill. Place 20 pounds charcoal in the pit and light. When flame has died, place pig on grill split side down. When charcoal has turned white, arrange it so that most of the coals are underneath the hams and shoulders, with a small amount under the rib cage. When coals begin to die, start additional charcoal outside the pit and add only live coals to the pit. Cook for four to six hours depending on size of pig. When the leg joints become stiff, turn the pig on its back and continue cooking for an additional four to six hours, basting twice with the vinegar and pepper mixture. An hour before serving, baste with your favorite barbecue sauce. To check for doneness, check hams and shoulders with meat thermometer. The temperature should reach 170 degrees before serving.

Remember, cook *slow*. There should be a heavier concentration of charcoal at the shoulder and butt end of the pit to cook pig more evenly. Serves a yard full of people (over 100).

ART SIEMERING

The Food Editor and Restaurant Critic for *The Kansas City Star* newspaper, Art Siemering's first job in the restaurant business was as a carhop. His next job was as a waiter. Eventually he stopped getting tips, and started giving tips—on food and restaurants to his readers. After writing about food for publications in Florida and Nebraska, he moved to Kansas City, where he devised a barbecue recipe for indoor/outdoor ribs that was so good it made the pages of the *Ladies' Home Journal.*

ART SIEMERING'S INDOOR/OUTDOOR RIBS

4 pounds pork ribs or beef short ribs
1/2 cup strong-flavored beer
4 tablespoons light molasses
2 teaspoons Maggi gravy seasoning or similar product (such as Kitchen Bouquet)
1 teaspoon liquid smoke
1 teaspoon sesame oil (no other oil will do)
any of Kansas City's own barbecue sauces

Place ribs in a large roasting pan. Pour beer around ribs and cover tightly with lid or heavy-duty foil. Bake at 400 degrees for one hour.

In a small bowl, combine molasses, gravy seasoning, liquid smoke and sesame oil; set aside. Remove ribs from oven; remove from pan and pat dry with paper towels.

To finish ribs in broiler: Place on rack, meaty side up. Brush generously with browning sauce mixed previously. Place rack four to six inches from heat; broil four to five minutes or until browned to taste. Turn ribs; brush with more sauce and broil.

To finish ribs on barbecue grill: Brush with browning sauce. Grill over hot coals for six minutes or until ribs are well-charred.

To serve, spread each portion over two slices of bread; paint generously with barbecue sauce. Serves four.

TOM LEATHERS

The publisher of *The Squire* and *The Town Squire Magazine*, Tom Leathers has a reputation for selecting the "bests" in Kansas City annually for his publications.

Might he consider his recipe for ribs—passed down from his mother, to his sister and finally, to him—a possible candidate for that special list?

TOM LEATHERS' INDOOR BARBECUED RIBS

3 pound slab of spareribs
liquid smoke
barbecue sauce

With a sharp knife, remove the membrane on the under side of the ribs. Remove all fat. Spread liquid smoke on both sides of ribs. Cover pan with foil and cook 1 1/2 to 2 hours or more at 275 degrees. Pour off most of the liquid in the pan. Spread your favorite barbecue sauce on both sides of the ribs. Continue cooking for another two hours at the same temperature until ribs are extremely tender. Remove the foil for the last 15 minutes. Serves three.

MRS. KITTY BERKOWITZ'S INDOOR BABY BACK RIBS

4 pounds baby back ribs
1/4 cup liquid smoke
1/4 cup tomato sauce
3/4 cup Old Southern Hickory
Smoke barbecue sauce
1 teaspoon salt

Place ribs in a baking pan. Mix all ingredients together. Pour over both sides of ribs and let stand one hour.

Preheat oven to 500 degrees. Place uncovered in hot oven for 10 minutes. Reduce temperature to 250 degrees, cover, and cook two hours, basting occasionally.

Remove to cool and serve. Delicious with an outdoor smoky flavor! Serves four.

MRS. KITTY BERKOWITZ

Mrs. Berkowitz informs us that she learned to barbecue at age 70—and has enjoyed it ever since! This is her indoor version of barbecued ribs which, from time to time, Kansas City's Mayor Richard Berkley has enjoyed.

BARBECUED SAUSAGE

PAUL KIRK:
THE BARON OF BARBECUE

Paul Kirk earned the title "Baron of Barbecue" from his friendly Kansas City barbecue contest competitor Dick Mais.

A former teacher-turned-chef, Kirk began cooking at the age of six and has a library of over 600 cookbooks—so you know he's serious. The owner of Molly Potts Chops and Chicken (see restaurant section), Kirk has won many cooking contests. He's been Grand Champion in the American Cancer Society's First Annual K.C. Championship Barbecue Cook-Off, Reserve Grand Champion at the American Royal Barbecue Contest and Professional Grand Champion at the Great Lenexa Barbecue Battle twice. Altogether he's won a total of 76 national, international and local cooking and barbecue awards.

Kirk has many secrets for producing some of the best chicken and brisket this side of heaven, many with a Creole influence.

"Sometimes I'll mix Wicker's wet marinade and apple juice or beer. Then I'll inject it and cook the meat at least 14 hours at 225 degrees and use my own sweet and spicy table sauce on it the last half hour," Kirk explains. "I also mix my table sauce with K.C. Masterpiece for a mellower flavor."

But barbecue isn't Kirk's only claim to fame. A creative cook, you'll also find Kirk's recipes for desserts and accompaniments in their respective sections in this book.

PAUL KIRK'S CREOLE SMOKED SAUSAGE

7 pounds fresh pork
2 large onions, minced
1 clove garlic, pressed
2 tablespoons salt
2 teaspoons black pepper
1 teaspoon crushed chili pepper
1 teaspoon paprika
1/2 teaspoon cayenne pepper
1 tablespoon parsley flakes
1/2 teaspoon allspice
1/4 teaspoon powdered bay leaf
1/4 teaspoon ground nutmeg
5 yards sausage casing

Grind the pork, using the coarse knife of a meat grinder. Add the onions, garlic and all of the seasonings and mix thoroughly. Regrind. Stuff into casings and smoke or barbecue. If this sausage is not hot enough for your taste buds, add more crushed chilis and cayenne pepper a little at a time. If you can, let the sausage sit in the refrigerator overnight. Also keep the sausage meat as cold as possible when making it. Serves 10 to 12.

GUY SIMPSON AND MARVIN DAVIS

Guy Simpson, owner of Accu-Rate Insurance Inc., and Marvin Davis, Executive Sales Manager with AT&T, recently teamed up to win a variety of contests. Among them, the Kansas State Championship in ribs, plus two second place awards for sausage and pork in the American Cancer Society barbecue contest. They also took first place in the sausage division at the American Royal barbecue contest.

SIMPSON AND DAVIS' BARBECUED SAUSAGE

4 pounds pork butts
4 teaspoons salt
4 teaspoons sugar
3 teaspoons sage
1 teaspoon nutmeg
2 teaspoons pepper
8 feet of pork casings

Have pork butts ground up coarse. Mix all ingredients with 1/2 cup hot water. Pour mixture into meat and work it in using your hands. Stuff sausage in pork casings and put in the barbecue oven on low heat (225 degrees) for 2 1/2 hours, turning once. Do not use direct heat for best results. Serves eight.

OTIS BOYD

The owner of Boyd's Barbecue, 5510 Prospect (see restaurants), Otis Boyd is a genial chef who can be distinguished by his ever-present red cap, which he dons to cook some of the best barbecue in Kansas City.

Boyd cooks his meat in a special pit that he designed. "I can smoke and barbecue at the same time," explains Boyd. "All my beef is barbecued—I cook it at the top of the pit at 325 degrees. In the middle are my ribs, which are cooked at 225 degrees. At the bottom is my sausage, which I slow smoke at 185 degrees.

According to Boyd the key to good barbecue is letting the smoke pass over the meat without allowing the meat to come into direct contact with the flame. The result is meat with a smokey flavor all the way through, and a slight pinkish color—something that makes Boyd's brand of barbecue so distinctive.

Boyd's most famous creation is his hot links sausage. After much consideration, he has decided to share his recipe with the readers of this book. His sausage, by the way, can be fried, grilled or smoked as desired.

Although Boyd has never competed officially in any barbecue contest, we think his recipe is a real winner.

OTIS BOYD'S FAMOUS HOT LINKS SAUSAGE

2 1/2 pounds ground pork
(shoulder cut)
2 1/2 pounds ground beef (brisket,
round or sirloin)
2 teaspoons sage
2 teaspoons red pepper pods
2 teaspoons paprika
2 teaspoons cumin
2 teaspoons sweet basil
2 teaspoons anise
2 teaspoons oregano
dash of salt and black pepper

Mix spices and meats together. If you want links, purchase 2 1/4" diameter casings from Fritz Meat Company and attach casings to a stuffer nozzle on a hand meat grinder. Fill casings with meat mixture to desired length, cut casings and secure ends with string. Barbecue at 225 degrees for two hours or slow smoke for four hours at 185 degrees. If sausage patties are desired, form meat and spice mixture into a roll and cover with waxed paper. Carve patties from the roll and peel off waxed paper. Patties can be fried or grilled. Makes five pounds sausage. Serves eight to 10.

RUTH DAVIS' BARBECUED SAUSAGE BALLS

**1 pound bulk sausage
1 beaten egg
1/3 cup bread crumbs
1/2 teaspoon sage**

Mix and form into small balls and brown in ungreased skillet. Pour off the fat. Add the sauce and cook together for 20 minutes on low heat. Serves six to eight.

RUTH DAVIS' BARBECUE SAUCE

**1/2 cup hickory-flavored K.C.
    Masterpiece barbecue sauce
2 tablespoons brown sugar
1 tablespoon vinegar
1 tablespoon soy sauce**

Mix ingredients together, pour over sausage balls and heat.

BARBECUED SEAFOOD

*NOTE: WHEN GRILLING OR BARBECUING FISH, ALWAYS SPRAY GRILL WITH VEGETABLE OIL *BEFORE* LIGHTING FIRE SO FISH WON'T STICK ON TURNING.

JESSICA KIRK

The recent Grand Prize winner of the Kansas State Championship, Jessica Kirk's prizewinning recipes for brisket, sausage, lamb and smoked catfish hooked the taste buds of the judges. Like her husband, Paul, she enjoys cooking immensely, and excels in the art of barbecuing. Mrs. Kirk prefers to use a dry marinade for many of her recipes and cooks by indirect heat, utilizing a portable "pig"—a 55 gallon smoker with a firebox for holding coals. A hole cut between the firebox and the smoker allows the heat to rise and slow cooks the meat.

"This is actually an old Chinese oven design," says Mrs. Kirk. "Chinese ovens work by indirect heat, also."

Using this process, Mrs. Kirk takes up to 14 hours to cook a large brisket; ribs, up to six hours.

JESSICA KIRK'S PRIZEWINNING SMOKED CATFISH

**one four-to-six pound catfish,
    whole**
salt
cooking oil

Clean, gut and oil catfish. Salt lightly. Oil a cheesecloth liberally and tie a knot in the bottom of it. Slip in the catfish, head first, and hang it with the tail end up in a smoker (see section on ovens) to slow cook for four hours. Serves four.

JAY COOPER

Popular Kansas City radio personality Jay Cooper lists among his many accomplishments, his ability to make a terrific barbecued trout. He does, however, vary from the traditional red, spicy barbecue sauce by using his own brand of barbecue heaven that he humbly calls "Jay Cooper's High Class Mustard."

"I'm talking about a mustard so fine that when your olfactory senses receive its essence, they sigh," he exclaims. "It is a mustard meant for sharing."

Unfortunately, Jay's mustard is in short supply. He and his wife Marcia make it in their kitchen for friends and family. The recipe itself is a secret, with the only copy locked in a safe-deposit box. It has a most unusual hot and tangy flavor and is guaranteed to unclog nasal passages in only one serving.

In the meantime, if you don't know Jay, you might try buying a sweet variety of mustard, such as Rooker's, or a Chinese-style mustard at your local grocery store. This type of mustard, by the way, has a wonderful way of tenderizing meat and adds a superior flavor to anything it touches.

As for Jay's barbecued trout, the recipe is best, he claims, when prepared at an altitude of 9,500 feet or more, preferably at Chapman Reservoir located above Basalt, Colorado.

JAY COOPER'S BARBECUED TROUT

1 trout per person
**1/2 cup Jay Cooper's High Class
     Mustard or a similar Chinese-
     style sweet and hot mustard**
1/4 teaspoon garlic powder
2 tablespoons butter
1/4 teaspoon salt

Mix mustard, garlic, butter and salt to taste. Clean and fillet trout and coat with mustard mixture. Lay coated fillets side by side on a grill over a low fire. (Make sure the grill is far enough away from the fire to let fish cook slowly). Baste fillets continuously with mustard mixture on both sides until done. Serve with mustard for dipping.

DICK MAIS' SMOKED TROUT

1/4 cup salt
2 cups brown sugar
3 cups water
1 stick butter
2 tablespoons lemon juice
two 8-ounce trout

Mix salt, 1 cup brown sugar and two cups water together and let trout soak in mixture for eight hours. Simmer butter, 1 cup water, 1 cup brown sugar and lemon juice over low fire until well blended. Baste the inside of the fish and the skin frequently while smoking over low heat. If trout has tendency to stick, try oiling outside of fish and wrapping in cheese cloth.

Note: Dick Mais recommends using apple and mesquite wood for best results.

CAROLYN WELLS' BARBECUED TROUT

1 trout per person
1 medium onion—ringed
1/4 teaspoon tarragon
1/4 teaspoon chervil
1 cup wet marinade, such as
    Wickers
1 tablespoon fresh lemon juice
1/4 cup vegetable oil

Split trout down the middle. Brush with fresh lemon juice inside and out. Place fish in shallow pan. Combine wet marinade oil, lemon juice and seasonings. Shake well in jar. Place onion rings under and on top of fish. Pour marinade over fish. Refrigerate one to two hours. Drain marinade. Cook fish over a bed of hot coals until done (15 to 20 minutes), basting frequently with marinade. (Also see section on wet marinades, as well as Carolyn Wells' recipe for venison and cornbread).

VINTAGE SWINE

Vintage Swine is a Kansas City barbecue team. All of the members are insurance company executives with Fidelity Security Life.

Headed by Jim Roberson, chief cook, the group recently won the Reserve Grand Championship in the Amateur Division at the Kansas State Championship in Lenexa, Kansas. They took first prize and Grand Champion in the miscellaneous division; first in lamb and third in beef. They also won first place in the miscellaneous division and first place in poultry at the American Cancer Society's Kansas City Championship.

Included here is their recipe for shrimp that won them first place and Miscellaneous Grand Champion at the Lenexa contest.

VINTAGE SWINE SHRIMP SAUCE

VINTAGE SWINE'S CHAMPIONSHIP WINNING BARBECUED SHRIMP

one 13-ounce can tomato sauce
1 cup Wickers barbecue
**   marinade**
1/2 cup brown sugar
1 tablespoon lemon juice
2 tablespoons Worcestershire
**   sauce**
1 to 2 tablespoons horseradish

Combine all ingredients in saucepan. Cook over low heat until sauce is reduced to one half of its contents. Serve with shrimp.

2 pounds jumbo shrimp
1/2 pound melted unsalted butter
1 cup Wickers barbecue
**   marinade**
3 cloves minced garlic

Clean, devein and butterfly shrimp. Combine with butter, marinade and garlic for several hours. Cook over hot fire for three to five minutes. (If cooked longer, shrimp will toughen). Serve with Vintage Swine Shrimp Sauce. Serves two or three.

AMERICAN RESTAURANT'S BARBECUED SHRIMP OVER KANSAS WHEAT

PRESIDENTIAL BARBECUE SAUCE

1 1/4 cups chili sauce
1 1/4 cups ketchup
1 1/3 cups tomato puree
1/4 cup diced tomatoes (canned)
    with juice
2/3 cup red currant jelly
1/3 cup tomato paste
1/2 pound veal bones, smoked
    with apple and cherry wood
    on barbecue grill or smoker
    until golden brown
1/4 cup fresh sage
1/4 cup fresh thyme
1/4 cup fresh marjoram
2 teaspoons whole black pepper
2 teaspoon cumin
1/3 cup dry sage
1/4 cup chili powder
1/4 cup paprika
salt, to taste
ground black pepper, to taste
2 tablespoons malt vinegar
1/4 cup onions, minced and
    sauteed
1/4 pound celery, minced
1/4 pound carrots, minced
1/4 pound garlic, peeled and
    minced
4 whole bay leaves
6-8 jumbo shrimp per person

Saute the onions, garlic, carrots and celery until tender. Place all of the ingredients into a heavy-bottomed sauce pan and simmer for 2-3 hours. Strain all ingredients through a strainer and hold for later use.

Use enough sauce to cover and simmer shrimp. Freeze or refrigerate any leftover sauce for use another time. Peel and devein shrimp after thawing. Place shrimp in sauce and warm by lightly simmering. Do not overcook or shrimp will get very tough.

(Makes one quart, can be frozen.)

Selected as a midwest representative in the "Taste of America" reception for the 1985 inaugural week celebration, the American Restaurant served more than 12,000 shrimp during the three-day period of this prestigious event. The holder of the Mobil Four-Star, Holiday-Travel and Cartier dining awards, the American Restaurant offers this taste of Kansas City-style barbecue.

AMERICAN RESTAURANT'S KANSAS WHEAT PILAF

2 cups hard red Kansas wheat berries—May be found in health or natural foods stores

12 cups hearty chicken stock (use necks and backs of chicken to enrich stock)

1/2 cup raw pumpkin seeds (toasted to light golden brown)

1 tablespoon and 1 teaspoon freshly-minced garlic

1 stick (1/4 pound) whole unsalted butter

2 tablespoons chicken glaze (see procedure for recipe)

freshly ground black pepper to taste

kosher salt to taste

In a heavy-bottomed sauce pan place the wheat and six to eight cups of chicken stock. Simmer slowly over low to medium heat, stirring occasionally. This is similar to rice pilaf, except that the liquid taken in by the wheat is far greater than that taken in by the rice. The wheat should be cooked till tender. (It will have a crunchier texture than that of rice).

While the wheat is cooking place 4 cups of chicken stock on the range over medium heat to simmer. This is for the chicken glaze. Simmer it till there is no more than 2 tablespoons of the syrupy mixture left—this is chicken glaze.

Place the whole butter in a skillet and melt. Add the garlic and cook for three minutes. Add the chicken glaze and stir to thoroughly mix. Add the cooked wheat, mix thoroughly, and simmer for five minutes. Season to taste with kosher salt and freshly cracked black pepper before serving. Serves six.

SERVING SUGGESTIONS

Use wheat pilaf as a bed under a shrimp dish, under a chicken breast, or with your favorite casserole.

KIKI LUCENTE

The owner of Kiki's Bon Ton Maison in the New Stanley Bar in Kansas City's Westport area, Kiki Lucente is one of the town's best kept secrets. Enraptured by the unique style of Louisiana cooking, Kiki began preparing Cajun and Creole dishes at her restaurant to the delight of customers, some of whom hail from Louisiana. They readily admit they are eating better in Kansas City than they could back home.

KIKI LUCENTE'S BARBECUED FISH IN CAJUN SAUCE

**4 pounds red snapper or bass
barbecue sauce—Cajun style**

Place fish on sheet of heavy foil and pour barbecue sauce over fish. Seal foil and place on grill with hood, if possible. Turn every 20 minutes and cook for one hour over a low fire.

Remove from foil and place on grill for 10 minutes. Turn and cook another 10 minutes, basting with sauce. Serves six.

KIKI LUCENTE'S BARBECUE SAUCE—CAJUN STYLE

**4 tablespoons oil
2 medium onions
3 cloves garlic
2 tablespoons parsley
3/4 teaspoons Louisiana Hot sauce
1 1/2 teaspoons salt
1 cup sauterne wine
1 small can tomato sauce
1 tablespoon lemon juice
3 tablespoons Worcestershire
    sauce**

Put onions, garlic, parsley, and Louisiana Hot sauce in blender. Add enough water to blend. Pour sauce into sauce pan with oil. Cook over low heat about 40 minutes. Add salt, wine, lemon juice, Worcestershire sauce, and tomato sauce. Simmer about one hour, covered, adding water if needed.

JIM FLYNN'S SOUTHERN-STYLE BARBECUED SHRIMP

1/2 cup chopped onion
1/2 cup chopped celery
1 clove garlic, minced
3 tablespoons salad oil
one 1 pound can (2 cups)
** tomatoes, chopped**
8 ounce K.C. Masterpiece
** barbecue sauce (red label)**
1 1/2 teaspoons salt
1 teaspoon vinegar
3/4 teaspoon chili powder
1 tablespoon Worcestershire
** sauce**
dash of Tabasco sauce
1 teaspoon cornstarch
1 pound raw, jumbo shrimp,
** cleaned**
1/2 cup chopped green pepper

Cook onion, celery and garlic in hot oil until tender. Add tomatoes, barbecue sauce and seasonings. Simmer uncovered 45 minutes. Mix cornstarch with 2 teaspoons water and stir into sauce. Cook and stir until mixture thickens. Add shrimp and green pepper. Cover and simmer until done, about five minutes. Serve over a bed of rice. Serves two or three.

RUBS, MARINADES, SAUCES

(NOTE: Unused portions of wet marinade and sauces may be stored in the refrigerator up to one week, or in the freezer for two or three months. Dry rubs may be stored longer.

(Also see Table of Contents for additional information on dry rubs, wet marinades and sauces).

COWTOWN COOKERS
(JOHN SCHLOSSER, HEAD CHEF)

Since 1983 John Schlosser and the Cowtown Cookers have won First Place in such barbecue competitions as the Kansas State Championship in Lenexa, where the group took First Place in the amateur category for pork. Cowtown Cookers came in first again at the Blue Springs Blaze Out in the amateur category for beef. The group has taken second and third place in a variety of regional barbecue contests, and plans to win more competitions in the future.

Says Schlosser: "We always start with the best quality meat available. We make sure the cuts are either choice or prime, and we don't trim the fat off before cooking. It's important to keep the meat as far away as possible from the fire. The heat from the smoke itself will cook the meat."

Schlosser's prize-winners utilize his own brand of dry barbecue rub (see recipe), which helps to seal the meat and keep it from drying out.

COWTOWN COOKERS' BASIC BARBECUE RUB

2 cups sugar
1 1/2 cups barbecue spice
3/4 cup salt
1/2 cup seasoned salt
1/2 teaspoons garlic powder
1/2 teaspoon paprika
1/2 teaspoon cayenne pepper
1 tablespoon mustard seed

Combine all ingredients and mix well. Sprinkle generously on meat and rub it in. Let sit at least 30 minutes before cooking.

PAUL KIRK'S BASIC BARBECUE RUB

2 cups sugar
1 cup barbecue spice
1/2 cup salt

Mix and blend well. Rub heavily on meat before barbecuing.

PAUL KIRK'S TEXAS BARBECUE RUB

1 cup salt
1 cup black pepper
1 cup paprika

Mix and rub on meat before barbecuing.

RICH DAVIS' BASIC DRY RUB

1/2 cup brown sugar
1/2 cup black pepper, coarsely ground
1/2 cup paprika
1/4 cup chili powder
1/4 cup salt
2 tablespoons garlic powder

NOTE: Feel free to experiment with these rubs. For example, you could take the salt away from one of the rubs, cut ingredients in half, or add seasoned garlic, celery or onion salts. Keep trying until you get the one that works for you.

DICK MAIS' SOUTHERN STYLE VINEGAR MARINADE AND BASTE

2 cups apple cider vinegar
1 cup K.C. Masterpiece red label barbecue sauce
2 tablespoons lemon juice
1 tablespoon dry mustard

Combine and simmer mixture over low heat until well blended. Cool. Cover meat and marinate up to 24 hours in refrigerator. This mixture also acts as a natural tenderizer.

DICK MAIS' CHICKEN AND FISH MARINADE AND BASTE

2 tablespoons Dijon mustard
2 tablespoons lemon juice
1 stick butter
1 teaspoon Lowry's seasoning salt

Combine and simmer mixture over low heat for 10 minutes. Cover chicken or fish for 30 minutes with the marinade. Use remaining liquid as baste.

AMERICAN RESTAURANT'S ALL PURPOSE NATURAL BARBECUE SAUCE (COURTESY OF CHEF KEN DUNN)

10 pounds chicken backs, washed and roasted to a dark, golden brown

3 onions, peeled and coarsely chopped

1 bunch celery, coarsely chopped

8 carrots, peeled and coarsely chopped

3/4 cup freshly chopped thyme

3 cups freshly chopped basil

10 bay leaves

3 cloves crushed garlic

2 cups Hunt's chili sauce

2 cups red currant jelly

4 yellow banana peppers

1 tablespoon whole black peppercorns

1/2 cup white wine, optional

2 tablespoons cornstarch, optional

Place the chicken backs in a heavy roasting pan and roast in a 425 degree oven until dark golden brown. Pour off grease from pan. Place backs in heavy-bottomed stock pot. Place vegetables in pan in which backs were cooked and put into a 425 degree oven. Brown well, stirring about every 10 minutes.

Add browned vegetables to backs and cover with cold water. Bring to boil over high heat, then lower heat, add herbs and seasonings, and simmer for six hours or more. Strain stock, and discard bones and vegetables. Put stock back in pot and add jelly, chili sauce and yellow banana peppers. Simmer for at least one hour. If the sauce needs thickening, add a mixture of white wine and cornstarch and cook a little longer.

NOTE: A nice variation on this sauce is to take the roasted chicken backs and smoke them on the coarcoal grill with hickory or apple chips before placing backs in the stock pot. This will add a natural smokey flavor to the results.

JEANNE BUNN'S BARBECUE SAUCE

1/4 cup chopped onion
2 tablespoons salad oil
2 cups ketchup
1/3 cup honey
1/4 cup Worcestershire sauce
1 teaspoon prepared horseradish mustard (or more, up to 1 tablespoon)
1/2 teaspoon liquid smoke
1 teaspoon vinegar
1/4 teaspoon garlic salt
1/4 teaspoon coarse-cracked pepper
1/4 teaspoon crushed rosemary
1/4 teaspoon thyme, crushed
1/4 teaspoon crushed oregano
1/4 teaspoon savory
2 drops Tabasco sauce

Cook onion in oil until tender. Add remaining ingredients. Simmer, uncoverd, 10-15 minutes.

Mrs. Bunn has been making this recipe for over 20 years and it still works every time!

COWTOWN COOKERS' BASIC BARBECUE SAUCE

32 ounce jar ketchup
1 cup dark molasses
1 1/2 tablespoons Tabasco sauce
1 1/2 medium onions chopped fine
1 large green pepper chopped fine
1/2 cup lemon juice
1 teaspoon garlic powder
2 1/2 tablespoons dry mustard
3 tablespoons vinegar
3/4 cup brown sugar
1/4 cup liquid smoke
1/4 cup Worcestershire sauce

Combine all ingredients in large pot. Use 1/4 cup water to rinse out ketchup bottle and pour into pot. Bring mixture to a boil, stirring constantly. Reduce heat and simmer until onion and peppers are tender (around two hours).

ART JACKSON'S BARBECUE SAUCE

32 ounces ketchup
8 ounces barbecue seasoning
spice
1/3 cup sugar
3 ounces Worcestershire sauce
3 ounces A-1 Steak Sauce
1 teaspoon black pepper
1 quart vinegar

Mix ketchup, sugar and barbecue seasoning thoroughly in a large bowl. Add vinegar, then pepper, A-1 and Worcestershire sauces. Stir until mixed well. Cook over medium heat five minutes (optional) and serve.

ACCOMPANIMENTS

DICK MAIS' BANDALERO BAKED BEANS

1 can pork and beans
1 can pinto beans
1 can red kidney beans
1 can butter beans
1 can navy or great northern
    beans
1 cup chopped onion
1 cup K.C. Masterpiece red label
    barbecue sauce
1 cup chopped smoked sausage,
    barbecued beef or pork
1 tablespoon liquid smoke
    (optional)

Combine all ingredients and bake in oven at 325 degrees for one and a half hours. If using leftover barbecue for meat base do not use liquid smoke. Serves 10-12.

STEVE STEPHENSON'S BARBECUED BEANS

two 1-pound cans pork and beans
1 can drained canned tomatoes
1 cup apple cider
1/2 cup ketchup
1/2 cup brown sugar
1/2 onion, chopped
2 tablespoons horseradish
1 tablespoon Worcestershire
    sauce
1 teaspoon seasoned salt
1 teaspoon dry mustard
1/2 teaspoon pepper
1/4 teaspoon Accent

Mix all ingredients in shallow three-quart baking pan. Bake at 350 degrees around one and a half to two hours. Serves six to eight.

JUDITH EPSTEIN'S NON-KOSHER INDIAN-STYLE BAKED BEANS

3/4 pound bacon
2 large (40-ounce) cans pork
    and beans
1/2 cup brown sugar
2 tablespoons minced onion
2 tablespoons chili powder
2 tablespoons yellow prepared
    mustard
2 teaspoons liquid smoke
1 cup barbecue sauce (your
    choice)
1/2 cup dark Karo syrup
1/2 cup molasses

Fry bacon until almost done and drain on paper towels. When cool, tear into small pieces. Pour off a little of the juice from the canned pork and beans (throw out the little pieces of pork fat from the can), and combine with bacon and all other ingredients. Bake for one hour and 15 minutes uncovered in a 325 degree oven, or in a crock-pot for six or seven hours on the low setting. Serves six to eight.

NOTE: Use these amounts as a guideline. You may want to use a little less or a little more, depending on your personal taste. If the barbecue sauce you use is spicy, you may want to cut down on the chili powder. If the sauce is smoky, you might want to use less liquid smoke. Taste as you go along and see what happens.

JASON'S FRIED CORN

**2 cans niblet yellow corn, drained
thoroughly
2 jalapeno chiles, chopped
(optional)
1 tablespoon McCormick Salad
Supreme (optional)
salt and pepper
1/2 stick butter or margarine
plenty of toothpicks**

Melt margarine in heavy skillet and fry corn and chiles together until brown. Add seasonings, salt and pepper to taste. Corn should be hot and chewy and stick to, and in between, your teeth, if it's made right. Use toothpicks wherever necessary. Serves four.

DICK MAIS' CORN ON THE COB

**1 cup milk
1 stick butter
6 ears of fresh corn
salt and pepper
paper towels
aluminum foil**

Shuck and clean corn. Soak 12 paper towels in milk. Butter, salt and pepper corn. Wrap in milk-soaked towels (two towels per piece) and cover each ear in foil. Place on moderate grill for 45 minutes. Do not place directly over fire. Serves six.

CAROLYN WELLS' CORNBREAD

3 cups cornmeal
2 teaspoons baking powder
1 teaspoon baking soda
1 teaspoon salt
1 1/2 cups buttermilk
1/2 cup Wickers wet marinade
3 eggs slightly beaten

Mix together cornmeal, baking powder, baking soda and Wickers. Add buttermilk and eggs. Bake at 425 degrees for 25 to 35 minutes. For thicker servings, use a deep dish nine inch by 12 inch pan. For crisp cornbread use a shallow pan or cookie sheet. (See also, wet marinades.) Serves eight to ten.

ANN'S SPICY JALAPENO CORNBREAD

1 package cornbread mix
2 eggs
1 cup water
one 4-ounce can jalapeno chiles, chopped
one 8 3/4 ounce can creamed corn
3 tablespoons chopped onion
4 ounces grated cheddar
1 teaspoon chili powder (optional)

Grease nine-inch square pan. Set oven at 425 degrees. Mix all ingredients together. Pour batter into pan and bake 40 minutes. Serves six to eight.

JAY COOPER'S BARBECUED ONIONS

**one large white onion for each
    person
aluminum foil
butter
salt and pepper
two strips of bacon per onion**

Place each onion on its own piece of aluminum foil. Rub onion generously with butter. Sprinkle with salt and pepper. Take two strips of bacon and criss-cross over onion. Wrap each onion individually in foil and cook directly over coals for around 30 minutes. Serve onion in its foil jacket.

(Also see Jay Cooper's Barbecued Trout)

RICH DAVIS' OUTDOOR BAKED ONION SURPRISE

**several large, flat-bottomed
    onions, enough for
    each guest
butter
1/2 teaspoon Lawry's seasoned
    salt per onion)
    or
oregano and sweet basil**

Trim off outer layers until onions are shiny and smooth. Cut off onion top, core out the center around one inch deep. Fill the cored center with a large pat of butter and Lawry's salt. Or stuff with oregano, sweet basil and butter. Be creative and use a mix of various fillings. Grease an aluminum foil sheet and wrap the onion tightly. Place onion in hot barbecue oven (300 degrees) and cook 45-50 minutes.

RICH DAVIS' DEVILISHLY GOOD BARBECUED EGGS

4 hardboiled eggs
1/4 teaspoon salt
2 tablespoons K.C. Masterpiece
   mesquite barbecue sauce
2 tablespoons mayonnaise
2 teaspoons finely minced dill
   pickle

Split eggs in half, remove yolks and mash, adding salt, barbecue sauce, mayonnaise and dill pickle. Mix well with fork and stuff egg half with mixture. Sprinkle finely chopped parsley on top. Chill and serve. Serves four to eight.

RICH DAVIS' DILLED NEW POTATO SALAD WITH DILLED MAYONNAISE

2 pounds small red new potatoes
2/3 cup chopped sweet white
onion
1/2 cup minced celery
1/2 cup minced dill pickle
1/4 cup chopped egg whites
(from 4 hard boiled eggs)
Lawry's seasoning salt
salt
black pepper
paprika
approximately 4-6 ounces dilled
mayonnaise

SALAD

Scrub potatoes. Cut in half with skins on. Boil in chicken broth until tender, but not mushy, approximately 15 minutes.

Pour off chicken broth (and save for a soup base.) Cool potatoes to handle.

In a bowl, add potatoes cut into bite size pieces, sweet onion, celery, dill pickle and chopped egg whites. Sprinkle lightly with Lawry's salt, and add plain salt and black pepper to taste. Turning gently, add mayonnaise until coated and moist. You may need to add a splash of chicken broth to moisten further, since salad should be moist. Place in serving dish, sprinkle crumbled egg yellow, dill weed, and paprika over top. Refrigerate two to three hours before serving. Serves six to eight.

Note: This recipe was one of several served by K.C. Masterpiece Barbecue Sauce Company at the recent Presidential Debate luncheon held in Kansas City.

RICH DAVIS' DILLED MAYONNAISE

2 egg yolks
1/2 teaspoon salt
cayenne pepper
1 teaspoon dried mustard
2 tablespoons vinegar
1 cup vegetable oil
2 tablespoons half and half
1 teaspoon dried dill weed
2 tablespoons fresh watercress,
**   if available.**

Beat egg yolks using blender. Add salt, and a sprinkle of cayenne pepper. Add dried mustard and vinegar while beating. Slowly add vegetable oil. When thick, add half and half, dried dill weed and fresh watercress (packed). When blended, add to potato salad and mix thoroughly to coat.

PAUL KIRK'S CREOLE POTATO SALAD

Served at his restaurant, Molly Potts Chops and Chicken (see restaurant section)

5 pounds red potatoes
1 medium onion, finely chopped
6 stalks celery, finely chopped
6 green onions, finely sliced
6 hard boiled eggs, mashed fine
1 tablespoon minced parsley
2 cubes chicken bouillon
1/4 cup white vinegar
1/4 teaspoon Louisiana-style hot sauce
1 pinch powdered thyme
1/4 teaspoon salt and white pepper
1 cup mayonnaise or salad dressing
1/4 cup salad oil

Boil the potatoes until soft, drain and cool until they can be handled easily. Peel and cut to desired size. Place in bowl, pour in oil and vinegar and mix well. Add onions, celery, green onions, parsley and eggs. Mix gently. Add the hot sauce, thyme, salt and pepper. Put the bouillon cubes in two tablespoons water and simmer. Pour bouillon mixture over salad and toss gently. Add mayonnaise and mix again. Serves 10 to 12.

LINDSAY SHANNON'S AVERY ISLAND POTATO PANCAKES

**1/2 dozen medium-sized red
   potatoes**
**2 medium onions, grated
   (optional)**
2 fresh eggs
1/2 cup flour
salt
pepper
1 stick butter
milk or half and half
**Louisiana hot sauce (You can also
   use Tabasco).**
additional flour

Boil the potatoes in a heavy pot until they are tender (poke them with a two pronged fork). Pour off the water and mash the potatoes, adding the butter, milk, flour, onion, salt and pepper a little at a time. Stick your finger in the potatoes to taste, add more butter, milk, salt or pepper if needed. Cover pot and put in refrigerator to chill. Put eggs in bowl, mixing in hot sauce (you be the judge as to how much), about three to five drops.

Once the potatoes are cold, mold into pancake shape, dip in egg/hot sauce mixture, dust with additional flour, put in cast iron skillet that has been greased with butter. Fry until both sides of potato pancakes have a crust. Serve hot with country-style barbecue ribs. (See Lindsay Shannon's recipe in pork section).

Serves four.

MOLLY POTTS DIRTY RICE

(Courtesy Molly Potts Chops and Chicken)

1/4 cup Wesson oil
2 cups Uncle Ben's uncooked rice
1 bay leaf
1 quart water
1 bell pepper, diced
1 red sweet bell pepper, diced
4 stalks celery, sliced
1 small onion, minced
1/2 small tomato, diced
1 clove garlic, pressed
1 teaspoon Worcestershire sauce
1 teaspoon crushed red pepper
1/2 teaspoon dry mustard
1/2 teaspoon white pepper
1/4 teaspoon cumin
2 chicken bouillon cubes
1/2 pound ground beef, saute
and season with salt and pepper
pepper to taste

To a three-quart sauce pan, with a tight-fitting lid, add the oil and heat until hot, then add the rice and bay leaf. Stir and saute until the rice is light brown. Add the rest of the ingredients, except the ground beef, bring to a boil and stir well to make sure that the bouillon has disolved. Cover with the tight fitting lid and turn the burner off. Let sit undisturbed on the burner for 30 minutes or longer. Before serving add the beef mixture and fold into the rice. Serve hot. Serves eight.

SERENA HAMMER'S CRIMSON SAUERKRAUT

two 27-ounce cans sauerkraut,
      including juice
one-and-a-half 10-1/4 ounce cans
      undiluted tomato soup
enough water to rinse can
1/2 cup brown sugar
3 tablespoons schmaltz (rendered
      chicken fat) or butter, melted

Combine all ingredients well. Spoon into a greased 3-quart casserole. Bake, uncoverd, at 350 degrees for 30 minutes. Lower heat to 300 degrees and bake another hour to hour-and-a-half. Towards end of baking time, add a small amount of white sugar to taste. Serves 10 to 12.

PAUL KIRK'S BAYOU HOT SLAW

1 medium head cabbage,
    shredded and chopped
    (2 1/2 to 3 pounds)
1 large onion, minced
1 large green pepper, minced
1 small sweet red pepper, minced
4 stalks celery, sliced thin
1/2 cup Wesson oil
1 bay leaf
2 tablespoons flour
1/2 cup sugar
1 cup water
1 1/4 cup white vinegar
1 teaspoon Worcestershire sauce
1/2 teaspoon white pepper
1/2 teaspoon dry mustard
1/2 teaspoon granulated garlic
1/4 teaspoon cayenne pepper

Put the first five ingredients in a large salad bowl and mix. In a sauce pan heat the oil and bay leaf, stir in the flour, but don't let it brown. Add the sugar and water, stirring until thickened. Pour in vinegar and the rest of the ingredients, stirring until you have a smooth, thick sauce. Cool to below 100 degrees and pour over the slaw. Toss and mix well. Chill and serve cold. If you want a hotter slaw add more cayenne pepper. Serves six.

VIRGINIA GREGORY'S COUNTRY COLE SLAW

1 medium head cabbage,
    shredded (8 cups)
1-2 medium onions, diced
    (2 cups)
3 tablespoons chopped, canned
    pimento, drained
6 tablespoons chopped, fresh
    green pepper
3/4 cup vinegar
1 cup sugar
1/2 teaspoon celery salt
1 heaping tablespoon of salt
1 teaspoon celery seed
boiling water (just to cover)

Mix together well and barely cover with boiling water. Let stand an hour. Pack into jars and keep in refrigerator overnight. Drain and salt lightly when serving. Serves six.

DESSERTS

PAUL KIRK

A recent finalist in the Rich's Whipped Topping Contest, Kirk's recipe for Peanut Butter Custard Cake came in 36 out of 7,000 entries. The recipe, in one form or another, has also won several national, state and local awards, including the Georgia Peanut Commission's Chef's Recipe Contest.

Kirk's unusual Sauerkraut Sour Cream Spice Cake won him second place at the Kraut Packers National Chef's Recipe Contest in New York. Aside from that, the gentleman is a whiz at barbecue, too. (See his recipe for Creole Smoked Sausage).

PAUL KIRK'S PEANUT BUTTER CUSTARD CAKE

2 packages plain gelatin
3/4 cup orange juice
1 cup crunchy peanut butter
1/4 cup flour
1 cup sugar
1/4 teaspoon salt
2 cups half and half
3 egg yolks
3 egg whites
3 tablespoons sugar
1 angel food cake (hard and
    stale)
1/2 pint heavy cream, whipped
1/2 cup roasted Georgia peanuts,
    chopped

Dissolve gelatin in orange juice. Cook peanut butter, flour, 1 cup sugar, salt and half and half in a double boiler, stirring until well blended and thickened. While hot stir in the gelatin mixture and egg yolks. Cool. Beat egg whites until stiff. Add 3 tablespoons sugar. Fold into custard. Break cake into bite-size pieces. Layer with custard in a greased mold or angel food cake pan. Refrigerate overnight. Unmold. Top with whipped cream and garnish with roasted and chopped Georgia peanuts.

PAUL KIRK'S SAUERKRAUT SOUR CREAM SPICE CAKE

2 cups brown sugar
1/2 cup shortening
3 large eggs
2 cups sauerkraut, drained and
 chopped fine
2 teaspoons ground cloves
2 teaspoons ground cinnamon
2 teaspoons all spice
1/4 teaspoon salt
2 1/2 cups flour
1 teaspoon baking soda
1 1/4 cups sour cream

Cream sugar and shortening. Beat in eggs one at a time. Add kraut and spices, blend well. Add the flour, baking soda and sour cream, alternately mixing. Put into a greased, nine-by-15 inch cake pan and bake at 375 degrees for approximately 30 to 45 minutes. Top with icing.

BROWN SUGAR ICING

1 cup brown sugar
1/4 cup heavy or light cream
1/2 cup butter, at room
 temperature
1 cup chopped pecans

Mix together the sugar and butter. Add cream a little at a time until icing is smooth. Spread over cake and top with pecans. Place under the broiler until icing starts to bubble.

THUNDER THIGHS' INDIAN BREAD PUDDING

2 cups sugar
3 cups hot water
1 teaspoon vanilla
2 teaspoons cinnamon
1 loaf egg bread (bakery-style
bread, not white bread)
1 stick butter
2 cups raisins
1 pound grated mild cheddar or
longhorn cheese
cream (optional)

Toast bread lightly and cut off crusts. Butter one side of bread and place buttered side down in greased nine-by-13-inch glass baking dish. Makes two layers of bread in the pan. Set aside.

Pour sugar into a heavy, deep saucepan over medium high heat, stirring constantly, until it melts and becomes a dark caramel color (about eight minutes). Remove the pan from heat, and taking care to protect against splattering, slowly pour three cups of very hot water in a slow stream into the melted suger. At first the sugar will sizzle and harden into lumps, but it will dissolve as the mixture is stirred. Keep stirring over medium low heat until it is all dissolved, and then add the vanilla and cinnamon, simmering for one to two minutes.

Sprinkle the raisins over the bread, and then sprinkle the grated cheese over the raisins. Carefully pour the sugar syrup over all, making sure that all the cheese is moistened with the syrup.

Bake in a pre-heated oven at 350 degrees for 30 minutes. (Do not let it get too done!) Serve warm with cream poured over if you don't mind a few extra calories. Serves 12.

MARILYN MOORE'S SWEET POTATO PIE

(Ms. Moore is the head cook at Molly Potts Chops and Chicken.)

2 1/2 cups sugar
2 sticks butter or oleo
1/2 cup milk
1 tablespoon baking powder
1/2 cup flour
1 tablespoon nutmeg
2 teaspoons cinnamon
4 large eggs
3 1/2 pounds fresh sweet potatoes
four 8-inch deep dish pie shells

Wash the sweet potatoes, pat dry and rub with butter. Put in a sauce pan, cover with water. Bring to a boil, turn down to a simmer, and cook until soft. Let cool until you can handle them. Peel and cut into 1/4 inch slices across the grain of the potato. Melt the butter, add butter, eggs and sugar, mix well and add to the sweet potatoes. Sift the flour nutmeg, cinnamon and baking powder. Stir into the sweet potato mixture. Pour into the uncooked pie shells. Bake in a pre-heated 350 degree oven for 40 minutes or until the filling is firm.

LINDSAY SHANNON'S
SWEET POTATO PONE
IN EARLY TIMES SAUCE

3 cups grated raw sweet potatoes
2 eggs
1/2 cup sugar
1/2 cup dark molasses
1/4 cup unbleached white flour
1/2 to 1 1/2 teaspoons nutmeg
    (depending on your taste)
1/2 stick butter, melted
1 teaspoon pure vanilla extract

Put potatoes, sugar, flour, eggs, molasses, nutmeg and vanilla in a large bowl, pouring the melted butter onto mixture. Stir completely. Put mixture in a cast iron skillet for best results. Bake at 350 degrees for around 50 minutes.

LINDSAY SHANNON'S
EARLY TIMES SAUCE

1/2 cup Early Times Bourbon (only
    Kentucky Bourbon will do)
1 quarter pound butter
1 cup sugar
1 egg

Cut the butter into small pieces then melt in a double boiler over hot water. Mix the egg and sugar in a small bowl and add this to the butter. Stir with a wooden spatula until the sugar dissolves completely and the egg is cooked. This will probably take about 2 minutes. Don't let the sauce boil. Take the pan and set it on the counter so the sauce can cool to room temperature. Then slowly mix in Early Times.

If you really have a sweet tooth, pour this sauce on a piece of your Sweet Potato Pone.

COLEEN DAVIS' WILD HUCKLEBERRY PIE

Crust
(one 9-inch two-crust pie)

2 cups sifted all-purpose flour
1 teaspoon salt
1/2 teaspoon baking powder
1 teaspoon sugar
1/2 cup oil
1/4 cup cold milk

Sift dry ingredients together. Pour oil and cold milk over dry ingredients all at once. Mix gently. Divide into two parts. Roll each part out between two sheets of waxed paper. Place one crust into pie pan. Prick dough and save second dough for top crust.

Filling

4 cups fresh wild huckleberries in season (or any fresh berries in season)
3/4 cups sugar
2 tablespoons flour
2 teaspoons quick cooking tapioca
1 tablespoon lemon juice
2 tablespoons butter

Mix well and place in pie pan. Cover with top crust, making small decorative slits in dough. Dot crust with butter. Bake at 450 degrees for 10 minutes. Reduce heat to 350 degrees and bake another 30 minutes. Pie should be golden brown with juice bubbling onto crust. Let pie cool and serve warm.

THE RESTAURANTS

For our restaurant section we tried to paint a fair and accurate picture of a cross-section of Kansas City's barbecue places. As in most major metropolitan areas a few of the establishments are located in parts of town that may be regarded as unsafe after dark. We recommend that you visit these places for lunch, or go with someone who knows the territory.

We didn't try to give a formal critique of each restaurant. Rather, we strove to describe the food, ambiance, the owners and their style—letting the facts speak for themselves. We asked several reviewers to give their input in addition to ours, and feel we've come up with lively overviews that

will make you hunger for Kansas City barbecue.

We avoided restaurant ratings simply because, when you are talking about barbecue, you're talking about individual tastes and the variety defies comparison. It's more a matter of preference, we think. Who's to say hot peppered barbecue is too hot? Or that a vinegar-based sauce is better than the tomatoey kind? However, if something struck us as really outstanding, such as great ribs, this was noted and the reason given.

So we leave it up to you, the ultimate critic, to decide which barbecue represents the best that Kansas City has to offer.

RESTAURANTS BY LOCATION

DOWNTOWN TO PLAZA (K.C., Mo.)

Boyd's Barbecue
Bryant's Barbecue
Gates & Son's Bar-B-Q
Harris Bar-B-Q
Jimmy's Jigger
Little Jake's Barbecue
Margaret's Finest Barbecue
Molly Potts Chops and Chicken
Papa Lew's Barbecue
Richard's Barbecue
Sammy's Barbecue
Sherman's Barbecue
Smoke Stack Bar-B-Q
Stephenson's Old Apple Farm
Three Friends Restaurant and Bar-B-Q
Winslow's City Market Smoke House

PLAZA TO 171st ST.

Keegan's Bar-B-Q (Martin City, Mo.)
Longbranch Saloon (Kansas City, Mo.)
Smoke Stack Bar-B-Q (Martin City, Mo.)
Sneads (Belton, Mo.)

EASTERN JACKSON COUNTY

Gates & Son's Bar-B-Q (Independence, Mo.)
Oscar's Bar-B-Q (Lee's Summit, Mo.)
Zarda Bar-B-Q (Blue Springs, Mo.)

CLAY COUNTY

Bobby Bell's (Gladstone, Mo.)

PLATTE COUNTY

Steve Stephenson's Apple Tree Inn (K.C., Mo.)

KANSAS CITY, KS.

Gates & Son's Bar-B-Q
H&M Barbecue
Porky's Pit Barbecue (also Bonner Springs, Ks.)
Rosedale Barbecue

JOHNSON COUNTY, KS.

Gates & Son's Bar-B-Q (Leawood, Ks.)
Hayward's Pit Bar-B-Que (Overland Park, Ks.)
Longbranch Saloon (Overland Park, Ks.)
Zarda Bar-B-Q (Lenexa, Ks.)

BOBBY BELL'S
7013 N. Oak (Gladstone, Mo.)
Open for lunch and dinner seven days
Call for hours: (816) 436-2917

Former Kansas City Chiefs linebacker Bobby Bell proved that there is life after pro-football when he opened this popular north of the river spot in 1980. The retired Hall-of-Famer traces his love of good barbecue back to his teenage years, when he worked as a carhop at a barbecue restaurant in Shelby, North Carolina.

Bell's former occupation is very much in evidence in the decor of the restaurant. Lining the brick walls are framed photos detailing the highlights of Bell's gridiron career. Sports fans can relive the glory days of the Chiefs' Super Bowl victory while they chow down on a variety of smoked meats from Bell's enclosed hickory pit.

The Huddle Plate is a good bet for those who want to sample several of the restaurant's best sellers. The plate comes with a sampling of moist, meaty smoked sausage, charred burnt ends of beef brisket and two ribs, all drenched in Bell's sauce, which can be ladled on with abandon because its primary emphasis is on the sweet, rather than the spicy. As with all dinners, the Huddle Plate comes with thick, wedge-cut fries, bread and a side dish.

Additional dinner selections include a combination plate with beef, ham and ribs or a larger portion of any one meat. Sides include baked beans in a thick sauce, flavored with chopped meats, creamy cole slaw, onion rings, tossed salad and corn on the cob.

On the lighter side, Bell offers beef, ham or combination sandwiches. The combo features generous portions of thin-sliced beef and ham served on bread or bun with a crunchy dill pickle spear. For those with less than linebacker-sized appetites, Bell features a chopped beef sandwich or bun. A child's plate, consisting of a small beef or ham sandwich and fries, rounds out the menu of this family-oriented restaurant.

Bell's burnt-end plate is a real winner. This is a large portion of meat cut from the end of a prime rib. Bell says the burnt ends are extra juicy but unfortunately the meat is available only when he can get it from suppliers.

The Southern influence is evident in the Bobby Bell Special, a beef sandwich served with creamy cole slaw on top. It meets with plenty of resistance from Kansas Citians who say it isn't barbecue at all, but Bell says that those true to the south praise this unusual offering.

To round out the menu there's a monstrous 32-ounce glass of iced tea to quench a barbecue-inflamed thirst. Bell also offers a true rarity: a five-cent cup of coffee

For convenience a drive-up window makes it easy for pick-up orders, but a leisurely dinner inside makes the trip worthwhile.

BOYD'S BARBECUE

BOYD'S BARBECUE
5510 Prospect (K.C., Mo.)
Open for lunch and dinner seven days
Call for hours: (816) 523-0436

Otis Boyd's place is the color of rib tips. The low-slung building is covered with fake brick, but the barbecue inside is the real McCoy. Here, the atmosphere is convivial and sometimes the old-fashioned juke box is cranked up loud enough for B.B. King to rattle the bottles in the Pepsi machine. The place has the feel of the old roadhouses of long ago—those beloved rarities that dotted America's highways long before the interstates snatched away all things worth remembering.

Plastic-covered booths line the walls, with a bar taking up one corner of the restaurant. A hand-lettered sign lists packaged liquor brands and prices for take-out.

A selection of beef, ham, chicken, ribs and homemade sausage is the bill of fare, along with standard side dishes that feature exceptional french fries—the kind made from fresh potatoes deep-fried in lard.

The kitchen has been the domain of Otis Boyd for many years. Here the master barbecuer does what he does best. He's been cooking since the age of 11, when he worked at a hotel restaurant in Fort Madison, Iowa. An elderly churchgoer introduced Boyd to barbecue at a church fundraiser and it was love at first bite.

Eventually Boyd took over the old man's barbecuing duties and launched his own career.

Boyd opened up his place in the mid-'40s on the corner of 12th Street and Vine and made a lot of friends who knew good barbecue when they tasted it.

Today he still turns out great hickory-smoked barbecue from the large oven that covers one wall of his kitchen. He built it himself and says he can smoke as well as barbecue.

Boyd makes his sauce, blending anise, chili powder and a hint of cinnamon into a combination of around 12 different spices. The mixture contains no ketchup and is rich and full-bodied with a sweet aftertaste.

In addition to making his own sauce, Boyd also makes a terrific sausage that brings in folks from around the area (see his recipe in the sausage section). A mixture of beef and pork, ground with sage and seasonings, the sausage is stuffed into casings, then smoked for hours in his hickory pit. The result is moist and meaty, with a deep smokey flavor that delights the senses.

Boyd would probably work happily in his kitchen all day long if it weren't for the fact that he has so many customers to feed.

As he puts the finishing touches on his sausage, another fan wanders in from the Zion Grove Mission Baptist Church parking lot next door and orders up a lamb breast. Dousing it liberally with Boyd's sauce, the man devours it all as the juke box wails "Don't Stop 'Till You Get Enough."

ARTHUR BRYANT'S
1727 Brooklyn (K.C., Mo.)
Open for lunch and dinner seven days
Call for hours: (816) 231-1123

There are those who claim that Arthur Bryant's is the best barbecue in the city and maybe even the world. Certainly it has captured nearly all the limelight as a Kansas City tradition. But, come on—is it really all it's cracked up to be?

Well, it depends on your point of view. Would you push away a sandwich like a mountain, piled high with hickory-smoked beef and ham, accompanied by some of the finest fries this side of heaven? Would you forego lean ribs bathed in a crusty sauce whose creation began in the 1930s and is one of the barbecue standards today? One thing for sure—you'll either like the way it tastes, or you won't. And, if you do, you'll find that you can't live without sampling Bryant's barbecue at least once a week.

Writer Calvin Trillin has penned odes of affection for Bryant's, calling it "the single best restaurant in the world." President Jimmy Carter raved about the food when he dined there a few years back, and it is not at all unusual for first-time visitors to make total gluttons of themselves.

That kind of thing has been happening ever since Charlie Bryant began serving ribs in the '30s. When he retired in 1946, his brother Arthur took over the business. Both brothers have passed on and the restaurant is now run by Arthur's niece, Doretha, a quiet, soft-spoken woman who runs the place a little differently. Bryant's is a little cleaner, and the beef is a touch leaner. Some people think the old "grease-house" image Arthur Bryant used to tout is gone—and with it the mystique.

Perhaps. But good food is good food, and you can't eat mystique, anyway. Today you still wait in line, cafeteria style, for that brisket of beef, burnt ends and fries cooked in lard. The blockman throws a slice of white bread on a plate and with both hands, seizes a heaping pile of meat and slaps it on the bread. He brushes on the grainy, intensely-flavored sauce, and tops the sandwich with yet another slice of bread. The fries are added as a last mark of superiority.

There's no lettuce or tomatoes, no Muzak, no friendly beverage counselors, no hanging plants—nothing to stand between you and your sandwich. It is left to you to perform the remarkable feat of wrapping your mouth around a massive four-inch high creation that's meant for two—or someone with an insatiable appetite.

The meat is cooked for several hours in a pit oven over a low hickory wood fire. Doretha Bryant supervises the operation, having learned the techniques from her uncle.

"Good barbecue should be slow-cooked, tender and juicy, with a hickory-smoked taste that goes all the way through," she explains. "To me, the sauce makes all the difference in the world."

GATES & SON'S BAR-B-Q

GATES & SON'S BAR-B-Q
1411 Swope Pkwy. (K.C., Mo.)
1221 Brooklyn Ave. (K.C., Mo.)
1026 State Ave. (K.C., Ks.)
10440 E. 40 Hwy. (Independence, Mo.)
2001 W. 103rd Terr. (Leawood, Ks.)

**Open for lunch and dinner seven days
Call for hours: (816) 923-0900;
(816) 921-0409**

There are those who feel more comfortable eating barbecue closer to home. Ollie Gates knows that, and so he's expanded his operations from 12th and Brooklyn to 103rd Street and State Line in his quest to bring urban barbecue to the suburbs.

"Barbecue doesn't have to be dirty, greasy and ugly," Gates once said. To prove his point, his restaurants combine the best aspects of fast-food eating: service, quality and economy without sacrificing the uniqueness of good Kansas City barbecue.

The Gates family has been part of the local barbecue tradition since George Gates bought his first barbecue stand in 1946. Despite a fire at one location and the loss of a lease at another, Gates stayed in the beef and ribs business until his death in 1960.

His son, Ollie, enlarged the prospects somewhat when he began making pathways into this growing industry. After running a few pits in the area through the '60s, the younger Gates opened a new restaurant in south Kansas City in 1970. By the end of the decade, Gates & Son's was operating five restaurants in the metropolitan area. What they might lack in atmosphere is made up for by the food served on the trademark red and yellow paper plates.

Gates' deep pit smoking process, used at all the restaurants, consists of a pit with hickory or oak wood on the bottom and a grate over the top. The seasoned meat is cooked by heat, smoke and steam, resulting in one of the city's most popular varieties of barbecue.

Sooner or later it always gets back to the sauce. Gates offers a peppery sauce to accompany its barbecue and has managed to market it around town at many local grocery stores. You can also carry it home from the restaurants.

Another Gates plus is selection. While some competitors offer mountains of meat in sandwiches that challenge the mouth, Gates breaks his offerings down to three categories: the single beef or ham for small appetites; the regular beef or ham for larger appetites; and the beef or ham and a half for serious eaters. Both meats also come on a bun with a side of fries. All sandwiches are reasonably priced and the variety of sizes makes them even more affordable.

The behind-the-counter help never fails to greet customers with a booming "Hi! May I Help You?" which is your signal to order. The line is quick, a boon to someone picking up beef or ribs to go.

Yet there are those who complain that Gates, as a chain, is a bit too slick and homogenized. But if all you want is a good, solid, stick-to-the-ribs meal, then Gates & Sons is uptown downtown barbecue that's hard to beat.

H&M BARBECUE
1715 N. 13th St. (K.C., Ks.)
Open daily for lunch and dinner;
closed Sunday
Call for hours: (913) 371-9524

When it comes to barbecue joints, there's always something extraordinary behind an ordinary facade. Take H&M, for example. The first thing you notice about this Kansas City, Kansas, spot is that it appears to be merely an old house. The second thing you notice is the sign: it says "Harris" barbecue. Don't let that confuse you. It's just that Grace Harris, the owner, (no relation to John Harris of Harris Bar-B-Q) never bothered to take down her old sign to match the new listing in the phone book.

The restaurant has been around for 50 years, with Grace taking over ownership somewhere in the '60s. In the summer her fresh vegetable garden enhances the outside of the house-turned-barbecue-haven. On either side of the walkway leading to the door, you'll see fresh tomatoes and onions, part of tomorrow's salads and sauces.

People come to Grace's place from all over town. She's famous for her "chicken sausage," a delicacy fashioned from ground chicken parts, stuffed in a casing and smothered with her own brand of spicy-sweet sauce.

The interior of the establishment isn't fancy, just a few formica tables and a chalkboard menu for openers. A weathered Art Deco bar has seen better days, but it still holds plenty of beer and liquor.

The day's menu can be anything from hickory-smoked ribs to chicken, brisket or neckbones. Grace's Creole mother taught her the intricacies of preparing special dishes such as the chicken sausage she smokes with hickory wood in her pit—a 50-year-old wonder, 15 feet deep, that belches smoke and fire and is capable of cooking up to 500 pounds of meat at one time.

Like an amazon, Grace can spear a slab of boneless spareribs in one swift motion and set it down on the kitchen counter without so much as a sliver of meat being lost in the process.

A typical meal at H&M could satisfy even the biggest eater. The spareribs fight for space on a plate crowded with smoked chicken, fresh vegetables, salad and real potatoes that Grace hand-mashes and scoops from an old metal pan.

If you want any more than that, she'll fix it on request at the restaurant or for special at-home events. A true original, Grace can cook all kinds of ways—from Creole to oriental and you can bet it will be prepared in a tangy sauce with an excellent flavor.

It's notable that H&M serves up more than food. In the back of the dining room is "Grace's Blues House," an all-night spot where blues music is on tap along with barbecue from midnight until the wee hours. But, unless you go with someone who really knows the neighborhood, we recommend only lunchtime excursions to Grace's place.

HARRIS BAR-B-Q

HARRIS BAR-B-Q
2401 Brooklyn (K.C., Mo.)
Open Tuesday through Saturday
Call for hours: (816) 231-8290

Ahh, the old days, when cars lined the streets of the neighborhood near Municipal Stadium. Baseball fans were lined up at Harris', buying slabs and ribs by the carload for picnic feasts during the long games.

John Harris cooked the orders while the employees parked cars in his lot. After the game, players dropped by to drink some beer and enjoy "barbecue at its best," as the sign outside boasts.

The old stadium is no more, but baseball fans with the Harris habit still stop by for Harris' smoked sausage and double decker sandwiches.

The sausage is laced with sage. The beef and pork is mixed with garlic powder and pepper, ground and seasoned again, then stuffed into a casing before it's slow-smoked in a hickory pit.

Sausage isn't the only homemade item on the menu. Harris makes all the side dishes and the distinctive barbecue sauce himself. He comes in each morning, builds the fire in the pit in the back of the narrow kitchen, starts smoking and preparing his tangy potato salad and rich, thick barbecued beans.

Harris loves his work and cares about his customers, running the place entirely alone, except on weekend evenings when he's open late.

He's been doing this for the past 26 years, since he converted an old filling station into his barbecue eatery. Sadly, there were no celebrations or festivities to mark his 25th anniversary.

Quality and quantity are two reasons why Harris has survived. Take one bite of his tender brisket and you'll taste barbecue perfection. But go easy on the sauce: it packs a walloping punch. Made with around 20 secret ingredients it's steamed before it's served on top of the meat and is spicy enough to tingle the taste buds. Harris also sells the fiery stuff to go, for those of you who would rather break out in a sweat in the privacy of your own home.

Harris' specials include smoked lamb shank and lamb breast. These succulent delicacies aren't available every day, so it's best to phone ahead.

The Southern-style stovetop chili, with or without beans, is always available.

Some of Harris' fans, a blues group called "The Nighthawks," liked his establishment so much they featured it on the inside of the album jacket, something Harris is proud to show customers who come from around the city to dine at this no-nonsense barbecue joint.

HAYWARD'S PIT BAR-B-QUE
11051 Antioch (O.P., Ks.)
Open daily for lunch and dinner
Call for hours: (913) 451-8080

If you prefer dining at a barbecue restaurant to eating at a barbecue "joint," head for Hayward's.

Legend has it that Hayward Spears first learned his secret method of smoke-curing meat from his dad back on an Arkansas farm. Years later, Hayward started out by building three smoke pits in his own back yard, experimenting to determine which pit would provide the best flavor.

A clone of the winning pit has been built at the restaurant, the second one Hayward has opened since he started business 12 years ago.

Hayward says he cooks eight tons of meat every week, buying top-quality beef and cooking on an oven that rotates the meat to different levels of indirect heat, assuring even cooking.

The baked beans with pork are smoked in the same hickory pit. The drippings form a smoky sauce for the beans.

Hayward's tart, honey-based house sauce is a favorite with families. It's not too tangy, so it won't set your mouth on fire; even the kids like it. Hayward's sauce is also for sale at the restaurant and at some supermarkets around town.

The restaurant offers everything a barbecue lover might fancy. Short ends. Long ends. Burnt ends. Wet wipes. Plus a variety of beef and ham sandwiches served on buns, as well as chicken and smoked sausage.

The food is served in pleasant surroundings that definitely have a suburban feel: a deer head hanging on the wall next to the world's largest matched pair of bull horns; etched glass table dividers; hanging plants; brass fixtures; background music; and a computerized mini-billboard that showcases a variety of messages. On weekends, you might catch Hayward's wife, Hattie, performing a solo piano serenade.

Hayward's prime suburban location is the big reason for the restaurant's booming carry-out and luncheon business. Hayward's caters to a busy clientele that operates on a tight schedule. Service is speedy because Hayward has 85 employees staffing his restaurant and catering service.

The restaurant is always crowded, particularly on weekends, so be sure to get there early to enjoy barbecue served up the way Johnson County likes it.

JIMMY'S JIGGER

**JIMMY'S JIGGER
1823 W. 39th St. (K.C., Mo.)
Open daily for lunch and dinner
Call for hours: (816) 753-2444**

In a country where fast food franchises make dining an eat-and-run experience, Jimmy's Jigger is an anachronism. It's got the stuff Hollywood loves: your friendly neighborhood bar and restaurant, and an owner with a heart of gold.

The place opened in 1933—the day prohibition was repealed. Back then it was called the Bigger Jigger, and Jimmy Bowers went to work there, finally buying the bar from the owner and officially changing the name to Jimmy's Jigger in 1967.

A likeable, jovial fellow, Bowers has had his profile immortalized in silhouette on the sign over the front door. Another profile hangs in neon lights above the restaurant booths. It's hard to tell which side of Bower's face is most handsome. Bowers himself admits neither is his best.

Actually the owner is one of the nicest reasons to visit the restaurant. He's usually on hand in the evenings to greet customers, many of whom have become personal friends.

With the University of Kansas Medical Center just across the street, the place is packed with medical students, nurses and doctors who come in for a friendly beer or sandwich. It is said of Bowers that he's made more student loans than the university. In fact, he's received an honorary alumnus from the school in appreciation for his kindness above and beyond the call of duty.

His place is just about everything you'd want in a neighborhood establishment. The drinks are good, the food is reasonably priced, hearty and plentiful, and there's room for everybody to have fun. Although it looks deceptively small from the outside, Jimmy's Jigger is cavernous. The first room holds booths where people in love can whisper and businessmen can discuss the stock market. Another room has tables and a giant television screen for sports fans. There's a bar for singles and a stage and dance floor with a band that plays music for listening and dancing on weekends.

The only thing Jimmy's Jigger *lacks* is a reputation for good barbecue. That's because it took Bowers a while to get things right and he only recently got serious about barbecuing.

"I'm just a babe in the woods compared to the rest of 'em," he says. "Hell, I used to get ribs that looked like they came off a dinosaur. No matter how much I cooked 'em, I couldn't get the fat off 'em."

His ribs now come from meatier, smaller hogs, and he serves them along with chicken, ham and beef that are smoked to moist perfection in a huge converted bread oven that comes equipped with a firebox on the side. He uses hickory and cherry wood in the smoking process, which gives the meat a superior flavor.

There are other offerings on the menu, including crisp, deep-fried potato chips as well as golden fries, carved from fresh potatoes and as long as the palm of your hand. A joke or two from the owner is on the house.

KEEGAN'S BAR-B-Q
325 East 135th St. (Martin City, Mo.)
Open for lunch and dinner; closed
Monday
Call for hours: (816) 942-7550

Barbecue at Keegan's is a family affair in more ways than one. The prices are right, the food is good and there's plenty of it.

Many people from around the metropolitan area visit Keegan's regularly. Once they try the unique sauce, they make the drive often. You can pour on as much of Keegan's eye-watering hot or mild sauce as you like from the squeeze bottles on the table.

The ribs and sandwiches arrive without anything on them and it's up to you to experiment with both flavors, but be sure to keep a water glass handy.

The waitresses here are some of the most amiable in the city, and many of them have been with Keegan's a long time. One has worked for the family for 17 years, staying with the business since the Keegans moved to this new location several years ago.

Some of Keegan's waitresses have their own regulars who call ahead to make sure their favorite server will be there when they arrive. But the best waitresses in the world won't draw a crowd unless the food is good.

At Keegan's you'll have no beef about the barbecue. Keegan stokes the fire in his three-level pit with green hickory wood. He slow cooks the top quality beef and ham for eight to 10 hours and the succulent chicken for about four hours.

You won't want to miss his combination orders of beef and ham tips. The hickory-pit barbecue is served along with fried shrimp, deep-fried imported French mushrooms with creamy horseradish dip, excellent cole slaw and baked beans. You can simply indulge till you bulge.

The restaurant has a homey feel to it. Janice Keegan greets you as you come in the door.

Bill and his son, Tim, usually are behind the scenes, overseeing the barbecue pit, and getting orders out fast.

While the restaurant is a bit farther out than many of the others, it's worth a drive to sample the friendly fare served here. Keegan's also has a party room downstairs with a separate kitchen facility for serving large groups. It's this personal touch that makes Keegan's a favorite place of south Kansas Citians.

LITTLE JAKE'S BARBECUE

LITTLE JAKE'S BARBECUE
1229 Grand; 1018 Baltimore (K.C., Mo.)
Open daily for lunch Monday
through Friday
Call for hours: (816) 421-9595;
(816) 283-0880

For a whole generation of Kansas City barbecue lovers, the name Jake Edwards is enough to send salivary glands into overdrive. At one time in the 1960s Jake Edwards' Old Southern Pit Barbecues dotted no fewer than five street corners within a multiple block radius in downtown Kansas City. A trip for back-to-school or holiday shopping also meant a stop at one of Jake's modest, lunch-counter establishments.

Though Edwards died in 1984, his barbecue legacy lives on at Little Jake's, operated by Edwards' son Danny, and his wife, Maureen. A visit to the restaurant makes it clear that "little" Jake knows what he's doing, having learned the barbecue expertise that made his father one of the best barbecue men in town.

As Danny Edwards tells it, Jake was born and raised in Rome, Georgia, where career choices were limited to chopping wood and picking cotton, neither of which seemed an attractive option to him. Jake migrated to Detroit to work on an automobile assembly line, but soon was lured to Dallas by a cousin who promised a place to live and a car to drive if Jake would help out in his barbecue restaurant.

It was in Texas that Jake learned the trade in which he would make his mark. He moved to Kansas City in 1938 and opened his place at 1018 Baltimore, where he built a faithful base of customers with his thick, hand-carved slices of beef and ham. Eventually his reputation grew and he expanded to several downtown locations. Though his empire dwindled after a bout with the IRS in the late '60s, Jake maintained the original Baltimore location and moved to a new site on Main Street, south of the Country Club Plaza in 1972.

At this place, Danny began his apprenticeship in barbecue, working after school and weekends throughout the years. He took over the downtown restaurant in 1980, moving the business to the present two locations. (The Main Street restaurant was sold in 1982, although the current owners retained the rights to use the Jake Edwards name.)

Danny still serves up the Edwards traditional and distinctive thick and tender slices of meat, cooked in a hickory pit and cut by hand on a large chopping block at the back of the restaurant.

Lunchtime conversations are punctuated by the sound of Edwards' knife slicing through huge smoked briskets of beef, his expert hands trimming off the fat before piling the meat on fresh toasted buns.

Danny says the secret to running a successful barbecue restaurant is a "whole lot of being there." He's there every day, pinching four-pound slabs of ribs at the meatiest spot to check for tenderness. He also mixes up a huge batch of thin but hearty sauce, which he characterizes as "sweet and hot, but not too hot." The sauce has a definite kick to it, owing no doubt to the chili powder and cumin that flavors it.

Chicken and side dishes of potato salad, cole slaw and baked beans round out the menu at this barbecue landmark which, by the way, will deliver to downtown area patrons during lunchtime.

LONGBRANCH SALOONS
Seville Square, 500 Nichols Rd.
(K.C., Mo.)
Call for hours: (816) 931-2755
Loehman's Plaza
8951 Metcalf (O.P., Ks.)

Call for hours: (913) 642-2042

Open daily for lunch and dinner.

"Our food may be terrible, but it's slow."

Only one restaurant in Kansas City dares to make that claim: the Longbranch Saloon. The message is posted on the wall behind the cash register at the Plaza location.

But don't be misled by the tongue-in-cheek talk. After all, the walls of the Longbranch are filled with amusing slogans and quotes from Walt Coffey, resident sage and co-owner with Lou Piniella of Yankee baseball fame.

Coffee likes to advertise their establishment as a "sleazy place for nice people . . . where the customer is always wrong." But the crowds that pack the Longbranch's two restaurants are right about one thing: this is a friendly place serving fiery barbecue and frosty mugs of beer.

"It seems when you eat barbecue, it's always more relaxed than when you eat sauteed mushrooms and caviar," quips Coffey, who traded in his high-pressure lifestyle as an auto dealer to open the business.

The menu gives you just two choices for hickory-smoked barbecue: meaty, small-boned ribs, or lean, thick-cut beef sandwiches. Either way, it's the right decision.

Coffey believes that the main ingredient in good barbecue is good meat. So he buys slabs imported from Denmark. The Danish ribs come from younger hogs, which seems to make the difference.

"A small bone is the key to a good rib. More meat than bone. To me that's barbecue," Coffey says. "You start with a real quality slab."

Coffey says there's no great secret to tasty barbecue, either. Smoke a high-quality cut of meat over hickory wood the right amount of time, and you've got it.

As far as sauce is concerned, he says, it's over-rated as an ingredient. He drew that conclusion after the Longbranch conducted taste tests to see what sauce patrons preferred and found that his customers varied widely in their tastes.

Coffey serves a concoction of K.C. Masterpiece sauce customized by his kitchen staff with additional spices. The results are hot and sharp without overwhelming the smokey flavor of the meat.

While Coffey is convinced that the "barbecue mystique" is a "lot of bull," he still thinks there is something special about it. It's what he calls his "Roundtable and Ribs Philosophy." And it was this belief that prompted him to run an ad for the Longbranch calling for "World Peace through Bar-B-Q Ribs and Beer."

The ad read: ". . . if world leaders would just sit down at the Longbranch once a month and have barbecued ribs and an ice cold, long-neck bottle beer, we might get to know and understand each other and not blow the hell out of everything."

Well, who's to say borscht and barbecue aren't right for each other?

MARGARET'S FINEST BARBECUE

**MARGARET'S FINEST BARBECUE
5900 Prospect (K.C., Mo.)
Open for lunch and dinner Tuesday
through Sunday.
Call for hours: (816) 361-4464**

Margaret's Finest Barbecue is one of a dwindling number of establishments that truly qualifies as a "Mom and Pop" operation. Margaret and Walter May, the husband and wife team that operates the restaurant, believe in keeping the business all in the family. Margaret handles the seasonings and sauces, while Walter, along with Margaret's uncle, supervises the smoking of meats. Each of the Mays' three sons takes a daily tour of duty behind the bar, serving customers at the counter or helping out in the kitchen.

The interior, reminiscent of a neighborhood tavern, is split into two sections, with a divider separating the dining room from the bar area.

The story behind Margaret's Barbecue can be traced back to the family gatherings at which Walter willingly donned a chef's apron to prepare smoked chicken, turkey and ribs for appreciative relatives.

With his reputation as a backyard barbecue whiz and Margaret's expertise in the kitchen, the idea of starting their own place began to take shape. They bought Sherman Thompson's old restaurant (see Sherman's Barbecue) in 1981.

Margaret now devotes all of her energies to preparing the meals at the establishment. She experimented for several weeks with a sauce that she felt would enhance the meat, and now serves this spicy combination that is a mix of pepper, garlic and other ingredients.

Walter devised a cooking process that enables the hickory smoke to permeate the meat without drying it out. He constructed a firebox adjacent to the restaurant's barbecue pit. The smoke is fanned from the firebox into the pit without allowing the flames to come into direct contact with the meat. The result is that all of Margaret's smoked meats, from the thin-sliced brisket to the succulent meaty ribs, have a deep, smokey flavor all the way through.

Margaret also serves larger hickory-smoked beef ribs, lamb shanks, and sausage, which she says is all meat and contains absolutely no fillers.

For those who prefer something other than barbecue, the restaurant has fried chicken, hamburgers and hot dogs.

The emphasis here is on quality, and the Mays say that nothing is served at the restaurant that the employees wouldn't eat themselves. They also confidently make the claim that if you aren't satisfied with your dinner, your food will be replaced or your money refunded.

MOLLY POTTS CHOPS AND CHICKEN
Harling's Upstairs
3941-A Main (K.C., Mo.)
Open daily for lunch and dinner
Call for hours: (816) 531-0303

Molly Potts is a tiny hole-in-the-wall place that sits far back from Troost in and among the hodge-podge of store fronts. You'd probably never notice it at all, if it weren't for the parking lot full of cars and people who come here at lunch time from all over town to sample the Bayou-flavored menu.

The restaurant is a mecca for neighborhood fans who know good food when they eat it. It's also a draw for uptown executives who dine here in Brooks Brothers suits and take home extra for dinner. According to owner Paul Kirk, one gentleman is so fond of his spicy fried chicken and "dirty" rice (a Louisiana favorite) that he travels once a month from Dallas to the restaurant and pigs out.

The place has only five tables for dining and most of the business is take-out. You belly up to the counter, where the jovial, bearded Kirk takes your order.

Heralded by friends as the "Baron of Barbecue," Kirk is a pro who's won many a contest (see his prize-winning offerings in the recipe section).

Proclamations and blue ribbons cover the walls of the establishment, declaring him Grand Champion in the American Cancer Society's first annual Championship Barbecue Cook-Off, Reserve Grand Champion at the American Royal Barbecue Contest and Professional Grand Champion at the Great Lenexa Barbecue Battle. In other words, the man knows his barbecue.

That's why when you bite into the tender, failling-off-the-bone rib tips you'll understand what all the fuss is about. The meat, cooked in an electric smoker rather than a pit, is not an expensive cut.

The rib tips are the top part of the rib—breast bone, gristle and fat—so they just sort of fall apart in your hands. But the subtly-flavored sweet and peppery sauce served over the meat makes wallowing around in the stuff very endearing. Besides, what would barbecue be without a lapful of napkins?

Rib tips and a side dish of Kirk's dirty rice (see recipe section) are definitely the way to go. The rice is a Creole creation that takes its name from the meat that's in it. In Louisiana, they serve the rice with ground-up chicken gizzards or livers. Kirk uses seasoned hamburger meat instead, to suit the tastes of his customers.

Other accompaniments include Bayou hot slaw, a cole slaw drenched in a hot sweet-and-sour oil dressing that is spiced with dry mustard, cayenne, red pepper and bay leaf.

There's also a spicy-sweet Creole potato salad that's excellent. (You can find both the cole slaw and potato salad in the recipe section.)

The restaurant also serves a Louisiana-style fried chicken, fired up with cayenne pepper and guaranteed to start a sizzle in your mouth. The "Pinky Wings"—covered by a ragin' Cajun sauce hot enough to turn your ears red—are for pros only.

OSCAR'S BAR-B-Q
601 N. Blue Parkway (Lee's Summit, Mo.)
Call for hours: (816) 524-6030

For the uninitiated, Oscar's color scheme and decor could be that of a fast food franchise. Nothing could be further from the truth. This family-owned operation prides itself on good homemade sauce created with loving care by the owners. The southern-style barbecue is pungent with a sweet and tangy taste, attracting a weekend crowd of hungry folks who wait patiently in line, ravenous for ribs.

The food, coupled with an ambiance replete with bull horns, beer signs, clocks and other memorabilia, makes a feast at Oscar's complete.

If you're one who tends to be skeptical about barbecue, you'll be tempted by the aroma that wafts from the doorway to the surrounding residential area. Like a moth to a flame, you'll be inside in no time, pigging out on a smorgasbord of beef, ham, pork, turkey and sausage.

There also are side dishes of potato salad, cole slaw, fries and baked beans spiced with the same sauce found in the squeeze bottle on the table.

The uniqueness of this concoction is what sells Oscar's to its many fans. You can't find the stuff in any grocery store, so you'd better purchase a couple of bottles here to take home.

The restaurant has a self-proclaimed reputation for being "the best anywhere around." A faded sign on the wall states, "No one can please everybody, but we try . . . that's for sure!"

Oscar attracts a large clientele, adding new customers daily from the eastern Jackson County suburbs. Family combination trays and children's sandwiches are a big draw.

Oscar has taken out the wall near the kitchen and put in a three-tiered oven where he smokes the meat. His sons help him, spearing slabs of beef from the depths of the pit and dropping meat into a bin to cool. The beef is refrigerated until it's ready to be eaten. For the final step, the slab is returned to the oven to finish smoking and goes from there to your mouth.

Feasting on the generous portions served here is a popular Friday night activity in Lee's Summit. Plan on standing in long, hungry lines on the weekend or during weekday lunch hours. But don't turn back. The food's worth waiting for. Best of all the price, like the meat, is appetizing to customers.

PAPA LEW'S BARBECUE
1509 E. 17th Terr. (K.C., Mo.)
Open daily for lunch and dinner;
closed Sunday
Call for hours: (816) 221-0379

Don't blink if you're driving along The Paseo in search of Papa Lew's. You may just miss it.

"I got to get me a big sign and hang it closer to the street corner," says "Papa" Lew Lyman, the owner of the restaurant bearing his nickname. He can be found most days working with his wife, Dorriss, in the little kitchen that produces such big meals.

Not too long ago Papa took a small, brick filling station on The Paseo and turned it into a modest barbecue joint. After cooking at an Italian restaurant for 20 years, there was little question that he had culinary talent. But he didn't know if Kansas City could support another barbecue restaurant.

"I felt like despite the other places with their years and years of business, I'd get my share if I knew how to run a restaurant well enough," Papa says.

The fire in his pit barbecue was lit in January 1983 for the first time and it's still going strong. By maintaining a temperature between 300 and 350 degrees, a brisket will be done in around four hours. Ribs, which take greater care, are usually ready in two hours or so. But to Papa, barbecuing is just a matter of watching the time.

"You got to have that touch of knowing when the food is done—the sense of feel you get with a fork when you punch that rib or brisket," he says.

Papa chooses a combination of hickory and oak for the fire and maintains his recipe for a mild, sweet sauce that enhances his brisket and ribs.

"It took me a couple of months before I got what I really wanted," he says. "But I finally nailed it down."

The specialty dish is the combination plate, a heaping selection of ribs, ham, beef and homemade sausage that will sate the appetite of most barbecue enthusiasts. Another special choice is the "Papa Lewburger," a hefty barbecued hamburger served on a steaming bun.

Papa doesn't expect everyone to eat *inside* his restaurant. That wouldn't be possible considering there are only three small tables here. There is an additional trio of picnic tables on the patio for dining in nice weather. The interior's only decoration is some brown paneling, which makes you think that Papa Lew is interested more in serving good food than offering swank trappings.

Word of mouth about his cooking has served Papa well. A steady stream of customers keeps the kitchen hopping at lunch, and the pace hardly lets up at dinner time. A stop here also yields more than the usual barbecue fare. The Lymans cook three different entrees every day. This could be anything from baked or fried chicken to liver and onions, and the barbecue. And for dessert, maybe peach cobbler.

"I wanted to do something other barbecue places aren't doing," Papa says. "People do get tired of barbecue."

But definitely not the kind of barbecue served by Papa Lew.

PORKY'S PIT BARBECUE

**PORKY'S PIT BARBECUE
4728 Parallel (K.C., Ks.)**

Call for hours: (913) 287-9688

**228 Oak (Bonner Springs, Ks.)
(913) 441-6297**

Open daily for lunch and dinner

Good Kansas City barbecue can be found in suburban as well as urban areas. Bonner Springs, for example, is 15 miles west of town, yet the people living here don't have to head for the big city to sniff hickory smoke or tear apart a short end of ribs.

After a successful debut in 1982 in Kansas City, Kansas, Porky's Pit Barbecue opened another restaurant in this community of over 6,000 residents. Although the two places operate as separate businesses, they are bonded by blood as well as purpose. Mike Woodhead runs the Bonner Springs establishment. He was trained in the barbecue tradition by his brother-in-law, Frank Hipsher, who works at the other location.

"It's quite a deal to know barbecue," says Hipsher, who cooked for more than 30 years at Rosedale's Barbecue (see review). Hipsher keeps a close eye on the brick pit barbecue at his restaurant, knowing there are few constants and plenty of variables in the cooking process.

"The weather makes a lot of difference on how the fire burns and how the temperature stays," Hipsher says. "One time your ribs might come out in two and a half hours, while another day it might take three hours. You just learn to tell how your ribs are cooking."

Patrons of Porky's in Kansas City, Kansas, can find a seat at any one of a dozen booths or grab a stool at the counter. A variety of barbecue dinners, including beef, ham, pork, chicken and ribs, are served with a pungent, spicy sauce. The meals come complete with side dishes of fries, slaw, baked beans and bread.

The specialty of both restaurants is ribs— long or short ends cooked to such tenderness they nearly shed their meat when you pick them up from the plate.

But the restaurants also serve more than barbecue: breakfast at Porky's in Bonner Springs starts at 6 a.m.

"One of the reasons we did that was because there was nobody else serving breakfast in town," Mike Woodhead explains.

In response to popular demand, Woodhead and his wife, Linda, offer turkey sandwiches, chicken noodle and vegetable soups, clam chowder and other non-barbecue items.

Still Porky's barbecue is the big draw. Right outside the front door is the big, stainless steel oven in which Woodhead cooks his barbecue slowly over hickory. The aroma is a terrific drawing card.

"To me this type of oven does a better job of keeping smoke and flavor and it runs more efficiently," Woodhead says. "But what makes the big difference is the sauce.

His brother-in-law feels wood is an additional factor in producing good barbecue.

"The wood is kind of like a spice. It enhances the flavor and it's just as important as the sauce," Hipsher says.

At Porky's you'll get the best of both.

RICHARD'S BARBECUE
6201 E. 50 Highway (K.C., Mo.)
Open daily for lunch and dinner
Call for hours: (816) 921-9330

If there were an institution of higher learning devoted to the finer points of American cuisine, Arthur Bryant would have been the undisputed dean of Kansas City's Barbecue U. It's clear that Richard France, the proprietor of Richard's Barbecue, picked up more than a smattering of knowledge in his 25 years of tutelage as one of Bryant's key employees.

France's barbecue apprenticeship began in 1955, when he arrived in Kansas City from his native Louisiana in search of work. An acquaintance in the unemployment office knew that Bryant was looking for someone to help out in the kitchen and suggested that France apply for the job. He was hired on the spot and began busing and washing dishes at the popular establishment. Eventually he worked his way up to meat cooker and counter man.

Bryant took a special interest in France, who soon became something of a protege to the master. He taught France that the key to good barbecue is not to hurry the meats during the cooking process.

France learned well. Today his beef briskets require 14 to 15 hours on the rack in an enclosed hickory pit, with ribs clocking in at four or five hours. He carefully checks the meat and, like Bryant, knows that timing is critical to the finished product.

But did Bryant pass along the recipe for his sauce? France turns cagey at the mention of this paprika- and pepper-laden creation that has both inspired and confounded imitators. All France will admit is: "Every time he made it, I was there."

France must have been a very apt pupil, judging by the taste of his sauce. The stuff looks like Bryant's own brown pepper and paprika concoction, but retains a fiery intensity not found in the original. It's also served from glass cruets, rather than squeeze bottles—a definite difference.

His restaurant, on the city's eastern fringe, offers slightly more upscale surroundings of brick and wood shingle. Nevertheless, France has duplicated the Bryant's experience right down to the familiar brown plastic dinnerware.

You place your order at a service window just inside the door and munch, while you wait, on crisp charred burnt ends. Just beyond the service area, a grease-blackened pit belches smoke as the countermen reach in to spear meaty briskets and slabs of ribs. The meat is finished off with a few slaps from a sauce-encrusted paint brush. You can finish off the meal by picking up a side dish of potato salad or cole slaw and a beer or soft drink on your way to the register.

The main dining room holds a table stocked with pickles, bread and silverware. (A knife comes in handy for subdividing the mammoth portions.)

Inside the dining room, tables and chairs are arranged around a portable television set, which on weekend afternoons is usually tuned to the Chiefs or Royals games, depending on the season. For some, dinner and a "show" at Richard's is one of the best ways to eat and enjoy in Kansas City.

ROSEDALE BARBECUE

ROSEDALE BARBECUE
632 Southwest Boulevard (K.C., Ks.)
Open daily for lunch and dinner.
Closed Sundays.
Call for hours: (913) 262-0343

Barbecue lovers are not known for standing on formalities. As any enthusiast will tell you, it's the quality of the food and not the amenities that make a barbecue meal memorable. For generous helpings of back-to-basics smoked meat and ribs, the Rosedale Barbecue has built a solid reputation as a purveyor of simple, no-nonsense fare for people on the go.

Nestled among the railroad tracks and warehouses of a largely industrial community, Rosedale's proximity to the downtown areas of both Kansas City, Missouri, and Kansas City, Kansas, makes it a popular lunch spot. A diverse crowd of business people and less formally attired patrons from the neighborhood mingle elbow-to-elbow, placing orders at the service counter at the midpoint of a spartan, L-shaped dining room.

The selections are uncomplicated: beef or ham, served on white bread or in a combination on long, hard rolls; ribs, short or long ends; and chicken, half or whole. Dinners are also available, with a choice of four side dishes: crispy, crinkle-cut fries; baked beans flavored with brown sugar and meat; cole slaw; and potato salad. Sandwiches and fries arrive wrapped in waxed paper, and table settings consist of styrofoam dishware and plastic cutlery. Canned soft drinks and draft beer complete the menu.

The meats are tender, sliced razor-thin and piled high on the bread. At age 80, owner Anthony Rieke still supervises the smoking process in a barbecue oven he designed himself, just as he did when the restaurant began 50 years ago, when it served beer and barbecue out of converted root beer stand at the same location.

In those days, Rieke cranked the rotisserie by hand. Today, he gets an assist from an electric motor.

Rosedale was established by Rieke and a brother-in-law as an alternative to working on a government funded WPA project in depression-ravaged Kansas City, Kansas. Having failed as a truck farmer, Rieke was determined to make a go of it in his new profession.

Employing trial and error, he refined his methods in a small, brick oven, prodding and basting the juicy meats until he was satisfied with the results. He's been feeding hungry customers ever since, serving up to 2,000 pounds of smoked meats on Fridays and Saturdays, when the restaurant does its briskest business.

Rosedale's thin but potent hot sauce is another of Rieke's creations. Rieke claims the sauce is a result of tinkering with spices, but he's not going to divulge any secrets.

Liberally applied to the sandwiches and ribs, the sauce complements, rather than overwhelms. Those of you who can't live without it can buy it to take home.

SAMMY'S BARBECUE
7044 Troost (K.C., Mo.)
Open daily for lunch and dinner;
closed Mondays
Call for hours: (816) 444-4561

Sammy's Barbecue has been a fixture at the corner of Gregory Boulevard and Troost for more years than current owner Jim Hamburg can remember. An agreeable, unassuming retired Navy man, Hamburg oversees the restaurant's kitchen and likes to tell about Sammy's former owner, the late Sam Bordman, who acquired Mammy's Barbecue directly across the street from the restaurant's present location. This was back in the '50s, when Sam didn't have a lot of money to spend revising signs and menus. So he simply changed the "M" in Mammy to an "S" for Sammy.

The restaurant changed hands several times before Hamburg bought the place in 1969. With a wife and eight kids to support on only his service pension, he needed a supplementary source of income. Hamburg admits to being a rookie in the business in the beginning, but a former employee taught him the ropes.

According to Hamburg, the secret of good barbecue is cooking the meat slowly for a long time. Hamburg uses hickory wood in his enclosed pit because he claims customers won't let him use anything else. The smokey flavor permeates all of his tender beef, ham and ribs.

Hamburg moved the restaurant from the southwest to the northwest corner of Gregory and Troost in 1980. The former gas station that now houses the restaurant has been converted into a cozy dining room with wood-paneled walls and comfortable booths. Strings of tiny Christmas lights frame the windows, casting a warm glow year-round.

You order the food at a service window, and it's delivered to your table a short time later. It's simple, but satisfying fare. The meat for the sandwiches is machine-carved and somewhat thicker than the razor-thin slices you usually get at other places. From the modest "Little Sammy" to the triple decker "Big Sammy," the meats remain moist and flavorful.

The ribs are good, too, and coated with plenty of rich, full-bodied sauce. Still made on the premises according to Sam Bordman's original recipe, the sauce is mild, with a pleasant aftertaste of celery salt.

For the first-timer, Sammy's Rib Combo dinner is a good choice. You can sample ribs, beef and ham on the combo dinner and pick out a favorite for future visits. All dinners are served with baked beans in a savory tomato sauce dotted with chunks of chopped onion. Standard dinners also come with potato salad and cole slaw, all with a stick-to-the-ribs goodness that has made Sammy's a favorite for so long.

SHERMAN'S BARBECUE

SHERMAN'S BARBECUE
8601 E. 63rd St. (K.C., Mo.)
Open for lunch and dinner Tuesday through Sunday
Call for hours: (816) 737-3110

Sherman Thompson is one of the grand old men of Kansas City barbecue. Thompson caught the barbecue bug as a child in Arkansas, and remembers watching his father prepare smoked beef and ribs over an open fire to celebrate summer holidays like the Fourth of July.

"We'd start the fire in the early afternoon and begin cooking around five and serve it the next morning," he recalls.

The passage of time may have dimmed the eyes but not the memory of this grand old man of barbecue who can recall a time when center cut pork chops were 15 cents a pound.

"If you had $5 worth of groceries, you could fill up your whole car," Thompson says.

The idea of starting his own barbecue restaurant began to take root after he arrived in Kansas City in 1931 at the tender age of 21. He had a cousin who was cooking barbecue in the basement of a joint at 16th and Woodland and selling his short ends for 15 cents and long ends for a dime.

"I got the idea, actually, from him. But I didn't do anything with it for a long time," Sherman explains. He held down a number of different jobs in area restaurants, but he put barbecue on the back burner until 1949, after he quit his job at the Missouri Pacific Railroad.

His barbecue was born in a small, one-story frame structure at 15th and Prospect. He adapted his cousin's cooking methods to an enclosed pit, devising his own special sauce from ketchup, white and red pepper, sage, garlic and vinegar. He mixed the excellent product in small batches and stored it in three-gallon jugs, then basted it on the smoked meats before serving.

A series of fires in the '50s led him to experiment with a new cooking method, which he calls "offset fire." This involved separating the cooking area from the actual fire, and eliminating the possibility of a grease flare-up when the meat drippings came in contact with a flame.

This idea was so successful, Thompson says, that many other barbecuers in the area copied it.

Thompson remembers selling between 1,200 and 1,500 pounds of meat on weekends alone at the Prospect location. Business boomed until an urban renewal project forced him to move in 1973 to 59th and Prospect.

Failing health caused the grand old man to pass the reins on to a new generation. After training his son-in-law in the family tradition, Thompson sold the place on 59th Street and the family moved the restaurant to its present suburban location. Sherman's daughter, Robbie Woodley, and her husband, Jim, are the proprietors now, but the food still has the mark of Thompson's expertise.

Woodley serves up the generous portions of beef, ribs and ham in a comfortable and spacious dining room decorated in a homey, Early American style. Wagon wheel lamps illuminate the dining area, which consists of booths separated by rustic wood dividers and coarse burlap curtains.

Beer is served by the pitcher in frosty mugs, and a separate cocktail lounge is open evenings. A private dining room is available if you call ahead for reservations.

SMOKE STACK BAR-B-Q
8129 South 71 Highway (K.C., Mo.)
Call for hours: (816) 333-2011

13441 Holmes (Martin City, Mo.)
Call for hours: (816) 942-9141

430 W. 85th (K.C., Mo.)
Call for hours: (816) 444-5542

Open seven days for lunch and dinner

Smoke Stack Bar-B-Q features state-of-the-art barbecue for its many fans. Barbecue historians might remember when Russell Fiorella opened the original Smoke Stack on South 71 Highway in 1957.

His pregnant wife, Flora, cried for six weeks because he sold the family home to buy the place, and they moved in above the restaurant and lived there with seven kids for many lean years.

Even Fiorella's creditors scoffed at the idea of a barbecue restaurant "way out in the suburbs" of Kansas City. And nobody would take a chance and extend him credit.

But he made it anyway, and today times have changed for the better. Now Fiorella is retired and three of his children—Jack, Mary and Carol—have taken over his booming business. Smoke Stack's barbecue today is one of the standards of barbecue excellence in the city.

There are now three locations, and each of the family-owned establishments has a unique, quaint atmosphere full of hanging plants and antiques.

Carol owns the original Smoke Stack, while Jack runs the Martin City location. And Mary takes care of the mini-Smoke Stack on 85th Street.

The small dining area at the latter location attracts a large lunch crowd. But customers also can order carry-out to save time.

The Martin City restaurant has the largest menu, with 36 imported beers available from which to choose. Jack's specialty is smoked fish, which his sisters don't offer. (Ask to see the separate menu for the fish. There usually are at least nine fresh fish flown in daily and smoked to succulent perfection.)

The meat here is smoked, with the tender beef ribs marinated in Fiorella's piquant sauce before being cooked in the hickory pit.

The mild, smoky sauce is tangy enough, but the spicier version has a real kick to it. All of the entrees and side dishes are worth trying, including the restaurant's excellent baked beans, made with chewy chunks of beef and ham, and smoked in the pit to allow the meat drippings to seep into them. Served in individual brown crocks, the smokey-flavored beans have long been a trademark of the restaurant.

A cheesey corn or potato bake, homemade cole slaw and colossal vegetable kabob are some of the other items offered that make you wish you could eat everything on the menu. There's always next time.

SNEAD'S BARBECUE

SNEAD'S BARBECUE
171st and Holmes (Belton, Mo.)
Open for lunch and dinner seven days
Call for hours: (816) 331-7979

If you're not hungry when you set out for Snead's, chances are you will be by the time you get there. Unless you're already on the southernmost fringes of the metropolitan area, the trek to this rural Cass County establishment is a long one. But the trip is worth the effort.

Traveling south on Holmes Road from Kansas City, you'll pass several blocks of rolling hills and lush farmland before you reach the unimposing one-story restaurant. The rural influence is noticeable in Snead's farmhouse-stylehominess, right down to the Mason jars filled with napkins placed on each table. The dining area is divided into two large adjoining rooms. The first has wood panelling and is decked out with stuffed deer heads. The second features large windows which open out onto several acres of rich Missouri farmland.

Bill Snead opened his doors on Halloween night in 1956. A concrete layer by trade, he had recently purchased the rural tract near Belton and planned to work the land himself. The restaurant was something of an afterthought, and Snead's friends gave the operation little chance for success because of its isolated location.

Snead proved his doubters wrong. When word began to spread of the superb hickory-smoked meats, city dwellers and country folk alike beat a path to his door.

Snead turned over the restaurant operation to Bill Eisen in 1978, but the high standards set by the original owner remain today. Eisen supervises the slow-cooking method, cooking the meat over an open pit fire.

Snead and Eisen believe that the flavoring of the food should be a product of the cooking process alone. For this reason all of the meats are served dry, just as they come off the grill. Eisen advises customers to check for the hickory-smoked coloration around the edges of the meat. If it isn't there, the meat hasn't been properly smoked.

You add the sauce at the table. It comes in two varieties—tomato-based with a surprisingly pungent aftertaste, and a milder, darker sauce.

One of the most popular meals on the menu is a plateful of Snead's "brownies." These are simply meaty burnt ends carved from the outer edges of the beef brisket and ham, producing a wonderfully chewy outer edge with a moist interior. Brownies are available on diner platters with thick-cut Texas toast and a choice of crisp fries, made from fresh potatoes, baked beans, potato salad or corn on the cob. A "sampler" plate consists of a choice of brownies, sausage, chicken and ribs and is one of the restaurant's best buys.

Snead's also serves fresh catfish, smoked and deep-fried and giant smoked turkey legs—two offerings rarely found anywhere else.

There's a three-beer limit with the dinners which is probably a good idea considering that it's a long way back home after a hearty meal at this country place.

STEPHENSON'S OLD APPLE FARM
**40 Highway and Old Lee's Summit Rd.
(K.C., Mo.)
(816) 373-5400**

STEVE STEPHENSON'S APPLE TREE INN
**5755 N.W. Northwood Rd. (K.C., Mo.)
(816) 587-9300**

Open seven days a week.

Most Kansas Citians are familiar with the fine hickory-smoked fixings that have made the Stephenson's restaurants famous. Lloyd and his twin brother, Les Stephenson, the family patriarchs, learned their trade back in 1932 as teenagers, when they worked for Charles Linville, who owned a barbecue joint right across the street from Stephenson's present location on Highway 40.

According to Lloyd, now 65, Linville's had an open outdoor pit and served sandwiches and ribs smoked over hickory wood.

"We cooked brisket of beef and pork butts all day long. That's how we learned," Stephenson says.

Eventually the brothers decided to go into business for themselves. In 1946 they talked their dad and older brother into leasing them the stone fruit stand that stood on the family-owned property across from Linville's.

"We sold our fruit in summer, along with fresh apple cider in the fall. Then in the winter we closed the windows and put in a little beer bar with groceries," Stephenson explains.

The business grew, and with it, the ambitions of the two brothers. They started adding on to the stone building and began serving what they knew how to cook best — country-style barbecue.

Today their style of home-cooking and gracious country dining has earned them the prestigious IVY award. The restaurant was also included in "Better Homes and Gardens' Famous Foods from Famous Places."

According to Stephenson, apple and hickory wood are utilized in a closed pit to smoke brisket of beef, pork chops, chicken, ribs and gizzards. The apple wood from Stephenson's orchards gives the meat a mellow flavor that is unique.

Stephenson's is a family-owned venture, with Les and Lloyd still overseeing the operations. Les helps out with the Stephenson's restaurant in Jane, Missouri. His son, Rick, acts as the manager of the restaurant at the Highway 40 location, and Lloyd's son, Steve, operates the restaurant on Northwood Road.

Les and Lloyd's brother, Norman, runs the orchards. The family grows its own fresh fruit in season, including peaches, strawberries and apples. And every bit of it is used in some form at the restaurant. You can order fresh-baked apple fritters, apple butter, hot apple pie with brandy sauce, fresh fruit daquiris and more. Plus gallons-to-go of fresh apple cider.

Complete with a bowl of lemon water to cleanse the fingers after a gala attack on chicken and ribs, a meal at Stephenson's is an experience to be savored.

**THREE FRIENDS RESTAURANT
AND BAR-B-Q
2461 Prospect (K.C., Mo.)
Open Friday, Saturday and Sunday
only
Call for hours: (816) 231-9753**

If the dining room at Three Friends Restaurant and Bar-B-Q weren't so large, you might think you were back home sharing good food with friends.

Jewell and Mattie Cornelius have a special knack for making you feel that way. The Louisiana-born couple work hard to make the restaurant top-notch, cleaning and preparing the food for weekend crowds.

They opened the restaurant in 1977 with four other couples, but eventually the partnership dwindled until just the two of them were left. With 25 years of experience behind her cooking at an Italian restaurant, Mattie relies on memory, not written recipes, and a keen sense of taste to tell whether or not a pie is ready for the oven.

Jewell, who retired from the Kansas City Southern Railroad, pitched in and helped his wife transform a two-story brick storage building at the corner of 25th and Prospect into their modest family eatery, keeping the high ceilings, and painting the walls a bright pumpkin color.

The barbecue on the menu at Three Friends is really a treat. Using a four-by-four brick oven fueled with hickory wood, Jewell cooks beef and ham, as well as pork ribs, for the half-dozen barbecue dishes the restaurant offers.

For ribs, the journey from pit to plate takes four hours. A brisket here is first cooked in a gas oven, then smoked in the pit—a process Jewell says helps the seasoning of the meat.

"If you put it in a smoker first, it won't season it that well. I think the gas oven helps tenderize it, too," he explains.

Besides serving sandwiches and combination plates, Three Friends serves slab ribs and rib tips. Although the slab makes good eating, the rib tips are really special. Cut into half-inch chunks they are a meal in themselves—especially when covered with the restaurant's thick, hot sauce.

A unique feature of Three Friends is the family-style service that makes taking a group of four or more a down-home treat. Just take your choice of meats—from beef and ribs to fried chicken, pork chops or catfish. Then order such extras as black-eyed peas and cole slaw, and you're in for something special.

"We fix it just like home," says Mattie. "All the folks just pass the plates around and help themselves."

Don't forget to leave room for dessert. A favorite here is Mattie's sweet potato pie, made fresh and served by the slice while it's piping hot.

Large groups are welcome, and if you've got 50 hungry people or more, you can arrange to have Three Friends all to yourselves Monday through Thursday.

The weekends are pretty crowded, and if there are no objections, you might be seated next to another party to make the best use of available space. Who knows? Maybe you'll leave Three Friends with more friends than you had before.

WINSLOW'S CITY MARKET SMOKE HOUSE
20 E. 5th St. in the City Market (K.C., Mo.)
Open for lunch six days; closed Sundays
Call for hours: (816) 471-RIBS

Don Winslow's reputation as the "Sultan of Smoke" is starting to spread like wild fire around the downtown business community. Free parking and fast service make the City Market Smoke House a favorite of the office lunch bunch.

Regular customers laud the merits of Winslow's slow-smoked meats. And Winslow is proud of the methods he's developed that make his offerings unique.

A massive brick oven, designed by an engineer, is located on the premises and does the job of slow-smoking very well. Not unlike Sherman Thompson's idea of "offset fire" (see Sherman's restaurant review in this section), the oven has the fire built in one end, with smoke traveling to a smoking area 14 feet away. The hot smoke, rather than the fire, actually does the cooking. The grease from the meat drips down and is collected at the bottom of the oven so that no grease splatters on the food.

Winslow also uses green, rather than seasoned, hickory wood.

"That's because green hickory gives off low heat and high smoke," he says.

Winslow also applies dry seasonings prior to cooking, using the best imported spices. The sauce, itself, is spicy hot with jalapeno and ancho peppers, onion and garlic. Fortunately the black strap molasses base extinguishes the fire a bit. Since the recipe calls for the freshest ingredients, Winslow makes up only two gallons at a time.

Finding the garden-fresh fixings is no problem, since his restaurant is surrounded by a market full of farmers peddling everything from tomatoes to herbs.

Everything at Winslow's is made from scratch, including cole slaw and the hot German potato salad with real bacon. The baked beans are made with smoked chunks of ham smothered in a rich barbecue sauce. Hand cut, not ground, beef is cooked in the same sauce to make Texican chili, another popular side dish served during cold weather months.

The "Smokie Joe" sandwich, one of the economical weekday specials, is composed of twice-smoked burnt ends, chopped and smothered in tangy barbecue sauce and is a year-around favorite. There are also smoked turkey, chicken and ham entries, plus ribs to satisfy palate and purse.

Winslow will also cater for special occasions. He does custom-smoking for several Kansas City restaurants and is proud of the fact that he smoked up hundreds of pounds of meat for the recent presidential debates.

"Since Kansas City is known as a barbecue town, I wanted to help extend that legend," he says.

ZARDA BAR-B-Q
11931 W. 87th St. (Lenexa, Ks.)
Call for hours: (913) 492-2330

Highway 7 and R.D. Mize Road (Blue Springs, Mo.)
Call for hours: (816) 229-9999

Open daily for lunch and dinner

If you're suffering from an overdose of fast food and you need a quick cure, Zarda Bar-Bar-B-Q has the panacea: great hickory-smoked barbecue. The friendly personnel at the self-service counter rapidly delivers your meal, no matter how long the line.

Mike Zarda and his brother Steve, co-owners of this restaurant and the one in Lenexa, have made barbecuing a science. Before opening the doors in Blue Springs in 1976, Mike experimented to find a formula that would allow for maximum smoke penetration of the meat, but with the least shrinkage and most moisture. The research yielded a water-injection system that ensures high humidity in the pit oven and a tender juicy taste in the smoked meat.

The pit oven in Lenexa is twice the size of the one in Blue Springs and holds 350 slabs of ribs on its ten shelves. The restaurant claims it has the "biggest cooker in K.C." But the huge size is necessary for the high volume of customers who come here for what Zarda calls "the biggest bar-b-q sandwich in town."

If you have a healthy appetite try a regular ham, pork or beef sandwich on a bun. The thick combo of two meats or a burnt end sandwich is also a filler-upper. Add a chicken and a half to the slab and you have the rib and chicken pack that's a complete meal in a box, including side dishes. For sissies there's a dietetic way out: the salad bar with soup and muffins.

But you won't find the smokey barbecued beans on any weight loss plan. Following an old family recipe, Mike doctors the hefty helping of beans with scraps of brisket and lets the natural smoke seep through. The smoke also gives the sweet molasses barbecue sauce a tangy taste.

The sauce, by the way, is a combination of 24 spices and every one of them is secret. Four of the ingredients are added in Kansas City, with the remainder blended in Memphis, Tennessee, and shipped—no doubt in a plain brown wrapper—to the bottler here.

Kids' plates, desserts, high chairs, big screen televisions and wet naps are clues that Zarda's holds great family appeal. But if you can't "come and get it," Zarda is happy to cater any special occasion. Carry-out also is available. If all you need is a quick fix of sauce, it's at most area stores and supermarkets.

MAIL ORDER

The following companies offer their products by mail. Call or write for more information.

SAUCES
Gates & Son Bar-B-Q
4707 Paseo
K.C. Mo. 64128
(816) 923-0900

Little Jake's Barbecue
1018 Baltimore
K.C. Mo. 64105
(816) 421-9595; (916) 283-0880

Kansas City Masterpiece Products
Suite 118
8340 Mission Rd.
P.V. Ks. 66206
TOLL FREE NUMBER: 1-800-255-0513 (outside the state of Kansas and the Greater Kansas City area. Major credit cards accepted) (913) 648-1282

Snead's Barbecue
171st and Holmes
Belton, Mo. 64012
(816) 331-7979 (major credit cards accepted)

Wicker's Barbecue Products
P.O. Box 126
Hornersville, Mo. 63855
In Kansas City call (816) 531-2620

Winslow's City Market Smoke House
20 E. 5th St.
K.C. Mo. 64106
(816) 471-RIBS

Wolferman's
2820 W. 53rd St.
Fairway, Ks. 66205
(913) 432-7130

Zarda Bar-B-Q
11931 W. 87th St.
Lenexa, Ks. 66215
(913) 492-2330

SMOKERS
The Recipe Exchange
3625 W. 50th Terr.
S.M. Ks. 66205
(This home-town manufacturer produces a converted chemical-free 55-gallon drum that can smoke up to 90 pounds of brisket at one time).

BARBECUE: KANSAS CITY-STYLE
AVAILABLE AT BOOKSTORES
OR ORDER TOLL-FREE:
1-800-255-0513
(Good outside the Greater Kansas City area and the state of Kansas.) Within the Greater Kansas City area phone (913) 648-0823. Major credit cards accepted.
If you want information on quantity orders for corporate gifts and promotional mailings call our toll-free number or write:
Barbecue Kansas City-Style
BARBACOA PRESS
P.O. Box 32576
Kansas City, MO 64111

SPECIAL BARBECUE GIFT PACKS

The following companies will mail order gift packs of barbecue sauces, products, and equipment made in Kansas City. Write or phone for catalog and brochures.

(Note: these companies feature *Barbecue: Kansas City-Style* as part of their attractive gift packages.)

Best of Kansas City
6233 Brookside Plaza
K.C. Mo. 64113
(816) 333-7900 (takes major credit cards)

Block-Pettit Gifts
P.O. 25544
O.P. Ks. 66225
(913) 451-9201 (takes major credit cards)

Masterpiece Specialty Foods, Inc.
Suite 118
8340 Mission Road
P.V. Ks. 66206
1-800-225-0513
(913) 648-0822 (takes major credit cards)
Attn: Ed Knight

River City Products
9504 E. 63rd St.
K.C. Mo. 64133
(816) 353-5558 (takes major credit cards)

SHIFRA STEIN

The former Restaurant Critic for *The Kansas City Star and Times* newspapers, Shifra Stein has had an ongoing love affair with Kansas City-style barbecue, taking time out from devouring ribs and fries long enough to write about it for many publications—including her own.

In 1978 she published her first book—a restaurant guide entitled *The Edible City.* So successful was this venture, that Ms. Stein continued to publish guidebooks including a local best seller called *Day Trips: Gas-Saving Getaways Less Than Two Hours From Kansas City.* The book was so well received that Ms. Stein was asked to create an entire *Day Trips America* series for East Woods Press of North Carolina. Garnering favorable mention in *Library Journal,* and *BookList* and a variety of other publications, the books are now available for St. Louis, Minneapolis, Houston, Cincinnati and Baltimore.

A woman of many facets, Ms. Stein's preoccupation with food and travel eventually earned her membership in the prestigious Society of American Travel Writers. She continues to write extensively for a variety of local and national magazines and newspapers.

Never one to stay far away from food, Ms. Stein admits she has put a lot of beef around her own ribs researching and writing this book.

DR. RICH DAVIS

Dr. Davis began barbecuing back in the '30's, learning from his father on a homemade grill and smoker. His natural talent and interest grew over the years, earning him first place awards barbecuing at the Annual American Royal Barbecue Contest in Kansas City.

Dr. Davis eventually developed his own sauce recipe and has gone on to create one of the fastest-growing companies in America—K.C. Masterpiece Barbecue Sauce.

A man of many talents, he has also been a family physician, Dean of a medical school, and a successful family and child psychiatrist. He has also maintained an active interest in food and wine as the owner of two delicatessens.

A man of diverse talents, Dr. Davis has written articles for publications ranging from a story on Kansas City barbecue for the *Ladies' Home Journal,* to a medical treatise for the *Journal of the American Medical Association.*

With over 40 years experience in the cooking and preparation of traditional regional barbecue, Dr. Davis has become a widely respected authority on the subject. Recently he and his wife, Coleen spent many months traveling around the country, sampling barbecue at restaurants and barbecue competitions across America.

"Each region has its own way of preparing barbecue, and it's all good. But to me, Kansas City barbecue and Kansas City barbecue sauces are examples of American regional cuisine at its finest," says Dr. Davis.